SOUND OF TRUMPETS

SOUND OF TRUMPETS

Faith Cook

THE BANNER OF TRUTH TRUST

THE BANNER OF TRUTH TRUST
3 Murrayfield Road, Edinburgh EH12 6EL
P.O. Box 621, Carlisle, Pennsylvania 17013, USA

*

© Faith Cook 1999
First Published 1999
ISBN 0 85151 778 1

*

Typeset in 10½/12pt Plantin
Printed and bound
in Finland by WSOY

To the memory of my father, Stanley Rowe,
missionary in China and Malaysia,
for whom the trumpets sounded in 1988.

*N*ow while they were thus drawing towards the Gate, behold a company of the Heavenly Host came out to meet them; to whom it was said by the other two Shining Ones, These are the men that have loved our Lord, when they were in the world, and that have left all for his Holy Name, and he hath sent us to fetch them, and we have brought them thus far on their desired Journey, that they may go in and look their Redeemer in the face with Joy ... There came out also at this time to meet them several of the King's Trumpeters, clothed in white and shining raiment, who with melodious noises and loud made even the Heavens to echo with their sound. These Trumpeters saluted Christian and his fellow with ten thousand Welcomes from the world; and this they did with shouting and Sound of Trumpet.*

from *Pilgrim's Progress*

These familiar words of John Bunyan will be recalled in these new biographical studies by Faith Cook. Her previous volume, *Singing in the Fire*, highlighted the perseverance of believers in the face of sufferings. Here we read of the conquests of faith in the lives of Christian men and women and of their triumph in death as the trumpets sounded for them 'on the other side'.

Contents

List of Illustrations

1. Colonel James Gardiner
2. Christian Watt, her mother and cousin
3. Archibald Brown
4. John Nelson
5. Dr Tom Barnardo
6. Samuel Pearce
7-8. The Wesleys' kitchen and music room

COLONEL JAMES GARDINER
Faithful unto Death

1

A young Scottish soldier lay wounded on a deserted battlefield far from home. Only surviving son of a godly mother, James Gardiner knew it could not be long before indisciplined enemy troops began to scour the area, stripping the dead of any items of value and killing those who appeared to be still alive.

Born in Linlithgow, west of Edinburgh, in January 1688, James Gardiner had soldier blood in his veins. His father, Captain Patrick Gardiner, fought first in the armies of William of Orange, who was to liberate Scotland and England from the arbitrary regime of the Stuart kings. Later he had fought against the French in the Duke of Marlborough's campaigns, dying in Germany from privation and exposure after the Battle of Blenheim in 1704. The loss of her husband, when James was only sixteen, was not the only sorrow his mother had known as a direct result of military conflict. Her brother had died twelve years earlier fighting in the Netherlands, and yet more poignantly, her elder son Robert had been killed on his sixteenth birthday shortly after joining the armed forces.

But nothing could restrain James from his ambition to follow his father into army life. Pugnacious from childhood, he carried throughout life a scar on his right cheek that he had earned in duel fought with an older boy when he was only eight years old. Nor had this been the only spar with his boyhood contemporaries. So, despite the earnest pleas of both his mother and his aunt, the boy became an army cadet in 1702 at the age of fourteen. He saw action almost immediately as Marlborough, anxious to break French domination in Europe in the War of the Spanish Succession, engaged the armies of Louis XIV, first in the Netherlands and then in 1704 at the Battle of Blenheim – the very battle that had cost his father his life.

In 1706 James Gardiner, now eighteen years of age and a junior officer, fought in the Battle of Ramilles, another of Marlborough's daring and dangerous engagements aimed at driving the French back to their own borders. Deputed to clear the enemy out of an advantageous position they were occupying in a churchyard, Gardiner and his band of brave compatriots were succeeding to some extent when a shot from a French gun hit him in the mouth. Numbed, he fell to the ground, and wondered vaguely whether he had swallowed the missile when he discovered that his teeth and tongue were undamaged by the impact. As Gardiner tried to trace the course of the shot with his finger he realised that it had travelled through his mouth and out of his neck, only just missing his spinal cord.

Evening of that long May day began to close in around Gardiner as he lay wounded at the scene of conflict. Then he heard the thud of running feet as Marlborough's own men pursued the fleeing French soldiers. But not a glance of pity did any spare the stricken man, so intent were they on clinching the position gained that day. Night fell, leaving James Gardiner alone with his thoughts, his anxiety and his pain.

Taught to fear God from earliest years, James knew that the preservation of his life was little short of a divine intervention on his behalf. For gunshot to pass through his mouth and out from the back of his neck without killing him outright astonished the young soldier. And if God had spared his life in this way, he must also intend him to recover from his wound, reasoned Gardiner. More than this, if he were going to recover, then he would need the gold coins he was carrying in his pocket. With this thought he struggled to secure his little horde of worldly wealth in his fist, hoping to conceal it from the looting French soldiers who would scavenge across the battlefield as soon as morning dawned. But no thought of humbling himself before his God as yet crossed the wounded soldier's mind.

By the time morning broke the effects of loss of blood and exposure to the cold night air had brought Gardiner to the point of death. He heard the French soldiers arrive to begin their looting and murder. And now someone was standing over him, having detected that he was still alive. As the looter raised his destructive sword to thrust it through the helpless figure before him, Gardiner heard the voice of another person close by, intervening on his behalf. 'Do not kill that poor child,' he remonstrated. And so the man passed on to his next victim. Unable to speak, Gardiner struggled to open his eyes, indicating his need of a drink. Having some spirits to hand, his benefactor, a friar, gently poured the liquor down Gardiner's throat.

After he had recovered a little, Gardiner made signs to the friar that he wanted to say something. In a scarcely audible whisper James told him that he had an uncle in a nearby town who would repay him richly if he would make arrangements to have him carried there. Although this was only a half-truth, the friar arranged for Gardiner to be placed on a handbarrow and wheeled towards the town he had indicated.

But the men who were transporting him lost their way in a wood, and by nightfall realised they would all have to spend the night in the open. With his wound undressed and rapidly becoming inflamed, the young soldier was in anguish. Each jolt of the handbarrow caused intolerable pain until Gardiner begged the men to finish his life themselves or leave him to die in the wood, where he would be free from the jarring movements of the cart. Faced with such a dilemma, the men decided to take him to a nearby convent where he would at least be treated with kindness.

The nuns received James Gardiner sympathetically and dressed his wound. When he had revived to some degree, the local barber attempted a little amateur surgery. Amazingly, Gardiner began to recover and within three months had regained his strength. Not only did the nuns show remarkable kindness to the stranger, but they also sought by their constant admonitions to convert him to the Roman Catholic faith. Although he was deeply grateful for all their care, Gardiner showed no inclination to accept their exhortations, nor indeed did he demonstrate any religious concern at all in spite of the unusual providence that had spared his life.

Restored to health, James Gardiner returned to Scotland in an exchange of prisoners and found himself honoured for his part in the Battle of Ramilles by a promotion to the rank of lieutenant. During the next thirteen years he advanced quickly through the ranks in recognition of exceptional service and bravery. Often in the thickest battle and in imminent danger, he yet escaped without receiving any further wounds. But through it all he gave no thought to his God.

The year 1715 found him serving in France once more where his duties often involved mingling among officials in the French court. There he became privy to a plot to remove the newly established George I from the English throne, and to install James Stuart, son of the displaced James II, in his stead. Within six weeks, so the rumour claimed, the throne of England would fall to the one who was to become known as the Old Pretender.

Without a moment's delay Gardiner set off for England to alert the armed forces to the impending invasion. The limited success of the 1715 Jacobite Rebellion was largely due to the alacrity with which Gardiner acted to defend his king and country. Riding swiftly northwards as soon as the invasion force landed, Gardiner reached Preston in Lancashire where the advance of James Stuart and his Highlanders was finally to be halted. Here with a small band of twelve men at his heels he dashed into action. Fearlessly he faced the onslaught of the enemy guns, setting fire to a barricade they had raised, while the shells fell all around. Eight of his heroic band perished that day, but yet again the life of James Gardiner was spared. These events brought him further distinction and he was shortly promoted once more, this time to the rank of captain of a regiment of dragoons.

However, all the achievements of the twenty-seven-year-old captain were marred by a dark and dishonourable side to his life – a side he would rarely speak about in after years, except with repugnance and shame. Throwing aside all the standards and instruction inculcated by his believing mother, James Gardiner flirted freely and continuously with any woman whom he could seduce by his winning personality and gallant appearance. Even his contemporaries who had not had his religious background shunned rather than sought out Gardiner's company, fearing lest they should be corrupted by him.

But James Gardiner was not entirely without checks and qualms of conscience. Once, as his companions were congratulating him on some particularly nefarious exploit, a dog entered the room. 'I wish I were that dog,' thought the unhappy man. Nor did he become a sceptic, throwing off all knowledge and belief in God. At the back of his mind he knew a day of accounting would come, and he would sometimes make attempts to pray. But he loved his sin and knew that he had no intention of giving it up. His understanding of God's character was sufficient to tell him that such a way of life was incompatible with his half-hearted prayers. And so he relinquished any further attempts at praying.

God's time was approaching, however, when he would intervene in the life of this dissolute young man. One Sunday evening in July 1719, having completed his duties with his troops, Gardiner, now a major, (for a further promotion had raised him to this rank), attended some function that did not finish until eleven o'clock at night. But Gardiner's evening was not over. He had arranged a secret rendezvous with a married woman at midnight. Having an hour to kill, he returned to his quarters, roaming restlessly around his room as the moments crawled by. With little better to do he picked up a small book that his anxious mother had concealed among his belongings. Being a military man, he found the title arresting: *The Christian Soldier, or Heaven Taken by Storm*, written by Thomas Watson, a well-known Puritan. Gardiner began to flip carelessly through its pages by the light of his candle.

Paying little attention to what he was reading, he was suddenly startled by a blaze of light resting on his page. Supposing it came from a guttering candle, he glanced up in surprise. The candle itself glowed with steady beam – but from higher up an unforgettable sight riveted him to the spot. There shining above him was a representation of the Lord Jesus Christ, dying on the cross. Radiating outwards all around were beams of glory lighting up the room. Hardly able to take in what he was seeing, Gardiner heard a voice speaking to him. Telling the story long afterwards to Dr Philip Doddridge, he could not be certain whether the words he heard were spoken audibly or whether they were merely impressed strongly on his mind, but he thought it was the former: 'O sinner! Did I suffer this for thee, and are these thy returns?'

Confounded, Gardiner sank back in a chair, scarcely able to move. How long he sat there he did not know. All remembrance of the sinful midnight engagement had vanished. Philip Doddridge continues the description as Gardiner related it to him:

Then he rose in a tumult of passion not to be conceived and walked to and fro in his chamber, till he was ready to drop down in unutterable astonishment and agony of heart, appearing to himself the vilest monster in the creation of God, who had all his lifetime been crucifying Christ afresh by his sins, and now assuredly saw by a miraculous vision, the horror of what he had done. With this was connected such a view of the majesty and goodness of God as caused him to loathe and abhor himself, and to repent in dust and ashes.

Scenes from the past flashed through Gardiner's mind: the earnest exhortations and prayers of his mother; the long night as he lay wounded on the battlefield; the intervention of the friar that had saved his life; the kindness of the nuns in their care for him; the many escapes from imminent danger. . . And against the backdrop of such a catalogue of divine mercies, he saw his own ugly way of life: the heedless path of unbelief and those sordid sins which had polluted his mind and body to such an extent that he had once declared he could never relinquish them unless God provided him with a new body. Without doubt he was a candidate for the just retribution of God's anger and for final damnation. Why God had not already struck him dead for his sins, he could not imagine. Before he left his room the following morning two things were clear to Gardiner. First, it could not be long before God dealt with him as he deserved, and, secondly, while he remained this side of hell, he would strive in some feeble measure to bring glory to the God whom he had so deeply offended. The thought that there might be pardon for his sins was as yet far from his mind. Gone was any inclination towards his former indulgences: such a manner of life now seemed obnoxious. In its place came a thirst for hearing the word of God and for secret prayer.

For three months Gardiner remained in this condition. Only then did he begin to entertain some hope that forgiveness was possible even to so grievous an offender as he had been. At the end of October 1719, God granted an assurance of pardon which flooded his whole being with joy. It came as he read the words of Romans 3:25–26 – words to be forever written in shining letters in his experience: 'Christ Jesus . . . whom God has set forth to be a propitiation through faith in his blood, to declare his righteousness for the remission of sins that are past, through the forbearance of God.'

Ecstatic with joy, James Gardiner, now thirty-one years of age, could scarcely contain his happiness. For three nights sleep eluded him as he felt 'the rapturous experience of that joy unspeakable and full of glory which seemed to overflow his very soul.' And yet, rising each morning, he felt quite refreshed as if he had tasted 'the noblest of cordials'. Clearly such a state could not last, and after these initial transports of spiritual relief and joy, Gardiner's frame settled into one of 'calm and composed delight' – a frame which was to mark his whole bearing for the following seven years.

The first to learn of his conversion was his mother, whose faithful prayers had followed her only remaining son throughout his years of ungodly living. And such a remarkable change in convictions and manner of life could not pass unnoticed by his associates. Some even reported that Major Gardiner was 'stark mad'. Never the one to duck a challenge, Gardiner welcomed the chance to demonstrate to his fellow officers the infinite advantages of a life lived to God. When invited to spend a few days at the country residence of one of the nobility, Gardiner asked his host if he might have the opportunity of addressing a company of officers and army men. His host complied, and a dinner was arranged at which they were all asked to be present.

After the meal Gardiner asked the men for a tolerant hearing while he explained the reasons behind the changes they had witnessed in him. He then challenged his associates to demonstrate in what way an irreligious and corrupt life style could compare with the joy and composure of a life lived in the fear of God. And if death should threaten, a fear often foremost in the lives of military men, what could be more desirable than a solid and unshakable certainty of a glory yet to come? Silenced by the force of his arguments that stood in marked contrast to all they had known of Gardiner's previous life, his fellow officers made no reply. Only his host spoke: 'We thought this man mad, but he is in good earnest proving that we are so,' he remarked thoughtfully. Gardiner's fearless testimony had won their respect, even if they might not wish to follow his example.

Not only did his fellow officers acknowledge the profound change that had taken place in the life of Colonel Gardiner, but the men over whom he had charge quickly realised that their commanding officer now demanded very different standards of behaviour from his troops. Discipline was strengthened, and soon the towns where Gardiner's men were billeted welcomed rather than dreaded their arrival. Swearing and blasphemy were prohibited, and any man who dared to offend was severely but fairly reprimanded. It was said of Gardiner that he feared the face of no man living where the honour of his God was concerned. But his men loved him. He cared for their persons, and if any were sick he would arrange for the best care available, coming himself each day to the sick man's quarters to enquire after his welfare.

His own personal discipline was well known among his men. Each day he would rise at five, for personal prayer and communion with God, before the duties of the parade ground or other assignments began. If some emergency required an early start on a forced march or other engagement, he would not allow his private devotions to intrude; rather he would rise yet earlier, in order to fulfil both commitments.

In 1726 James Gardiner married Lady Frances Erskine. They established a base in London, where their household could attend the ministry of the well-known Dissenting minister and historian of the Puritans, Dr Edmund Calamy. Lady Frances proved a steady and godly support to her soldier husband, her only fault in his eyes being that 'she valued and loved him more than he deserved.' His frequent absences from home, as the army was ordered from place to place in Britain and on the Continent, meant that she was often left to bear the responsibilities of her numerous family alone. Of the thirteen infants born to James Gardiner and Lady Frances, only five lived beyond early childhood.

Much as Lady Frances regretted the long periods of separation, frequent letters from him partly compensated. In these, written only for her eyes, her husband expressed something of his devotion to Christ, and allowed a curtain to be drawn aside on some of the unusual disclosures of the love of God which he was privileged to enjoy. 'What would I have given this day upon the road for paper, pen and ink, when the Spirit of the Most High rested upon me. O to declare what God hath done this day for my soul. Were I to give you an account of the many favours my God hath loaded me with since I parted with you, I must have taken up many days in nothing but writing.'

Not always did this devoted Christian soldier know such elevated experiences of the love of God poured out in his heart. During his first seven years as a believer such times were often his privilege, but after that he would grieve over the barrenness and deadness that sometimes clouded his spirit. Writing to Philip Doddridge he lamented, 'Much do I stand in need of every help to awaken me out of that spiritual deadness which seizes me so often. Once indeed it was quite otherwise with me, and that for many years; and here lies my sin and my folly.'

When Gardiner first met Dr Philip Doddridge, an immediate rapport between the two men sparked off a friendship of unusual depth and quality enriching the lives of both. It began in June 1739 when Gardiner, now raised to the rank of colonel, was listening to Doddridge preach in Leicester. Taking for his text Psalm 119:158, Doddridge described the grief of the godly man as he witnessed the bold and shameless arrogance of unbelievers in spite of God's righteous demands. Without knowing it, he was touching on a theme which had often exercised the army officer sitting in the congregation. But when he enlarged on the pity and tender compassion of God towards offenders, he was in tune with some of Gardiner's deepest sensitivities.

Hurrying into the vestry at the close of the service, this dignified military man embraced Doddridge with all the warmth of an old confidant. Long acquainted with Doddridge's writings, Gardiner did indeed feel he had at last met a long-cherished friend. After spending some hours together that evening and the following morning, the two parted. As Doddridge rode alone back to Northampton, he recorded how glad he was of these hours of solitude on his journey to ponder the delights of this newfound friend-ship.

Over the following few years the bond deepened. Some characteristics of his soldier friend particularly impressed Doddridge. These he was later to include in a short memoir published after Gardiner's untimely death in 1745. Among them were the deep joys the colonel evidenced as he attended the Lord's Supper. Tears would stream down the soldier's battle-scarred face as he thought of the love of Christ to unworthy sinners. And towards those whom he considered his friends, Gardiner would display a constant loyalty, always vindicating their reputation if any adverse comment reached his ears. Slander was despicable in his view, and he would never fail to reprove anyone whom he felt to be guilty of it.

Nor was Doddridge by any means the only one to appreciate the remarkable work of grace in Colonel Gardiner. The Countess of Huntingdon, whose social position and fervent zeal for the extension of the gospel was giving her an increasing role in the evangelical revival, was also quick to recognise the qualities of Christian zeal and commitment so clearly demonstrated in his life. Writing of him she exclaimed:

I cannot express how much I esteem that most excellent man, Colonel Gardiner. What love and mercy has God shown in snatching him as a brand from the burning! He is truly alive to God and pleads nothing but the plea of the publican, 'God be merciful to me a sinner'. What a monument of his mercy, grace and love! To glorify God and serve him with all his ransomed powers is now his only aim.

In their family Colonel Gardiner and Lady Frances faced repeated sorrows as eight of their children were taken from them in death. In one instance, Gardiner had just posted a letter to his wife expressing his relief at hearing that his young son was recovering from smallpox. But a moment or two later he received news that the child had died. Hastily he wrote again to his grieving wife, 'Your resignation to the will of God gives me more joy than the death of the child has given me sorrow. He, to be sure, is happy and we shall go to him . . . O what reason have we to long for that glorious day.' But the bereavement that cut both Gardiner and his wife to the quick was the sudden death of a cheerful six-year-old son, a child of unusual promise. Friends wondered how the parents would cope with such a loss, but God gave them the grace to triumph even here, as they reflected together on the evil world from which their child had been snatched, the snares and temptations from which he had been delivered, and the safety that now surrounded and protected him forever.

But such events, and the constant danger to which he was exposed in his vocation, caused Colonel Gardiner to meditate frequently on the glories that awaited believers in a better world. 'Oh eternity, eternity! What a wonderful thought is eternity,' he exclaimed in a letter to Doddridge. There 'all complaints shall be for ever banished, and no mountains shall separate between God and our souls.' Perhaps it was thoughts such as these that filled Gardiner's mind as he led his men hurriedly to Scotland in August 1745 in response to the alarming news of a second Jacobite invasion.

The government under the leadership of Sir Robert Walpole had adopted a *laissez-faire attitude to* any rumours of a further Jacobite rebellion. Even an abortive incursion early in 1744, when advanced contingents of the invading troops had been intercepted at sea and turned back, failed to place the army on full battle alert. Political uncertainties following the fall of Walpole from power, combined with military engagements on the Continent, found England ill-prepared to face an invasion. So when Charles Edward Stuart, the dashing and chivalrous twenty-five-year-old son of the Old Pretender, landed in Scotland the following year spearheading an invasion to claim back the throne, the military was caught unawares. Most of the army was billeted abroad, and little had been done to gather its forces in full strength. Not until the rebellious hordes swept down from the Highlands capturing towns and cities on their victorious way was any serious resistance mustered to counter the offensive.

Lady Frances and her eldest daughter were already in Stirling, and it must have been a comfort to James Gardiner as he led his men northwards to know they were there. By the time Sir John Cope, the Commander-in-Chief, and his troops arrived at Dunbar having sailed from Inverness, Edinburgh had already fallen to the rebels. Taking leave of his wife before he set off to prepare his regiment of dragoons for hostilities, Gardiner seemed surprised when she burst into tears and clung to him. He asked her why she was so distressed, for such situations were common in their experience. 'I fear I will lose you,' was her tearful response. But instead of comforting her in terms of the providence of God as he had done so often in the past, he replied simply, 'We have an eternity to spend together.'

Never a man to turn back in face of impending danger, Colonel Gardiner recognised that the army was likely to be defeated in the forthcoming engagement. 'I have one life to sacrifice to my country's safety,' he declared, 'and I shall not spare it.' But he had not the same confidence concerning the commitment of the men placed under his leadership. It had been many years since they had seen action, and they were untried in the face of a threatening situation. The rebels, on the other hand, were in an exultant and dangerous mood. With four and a half thousand infantrymen and four hundred horses, they felt themselves invincible.

As the armies drew into battle formation at Prestonpans, just outside Edinburgh, Gardiner rode in and out among his men exhorting them to fight courageously for their king and country. Their cause was right and good and the prosperity of the Christian church would be imperilled if the Stuarts once more gained the throne of England. This terrain was home ground for Gardiner, for he had been born not ten miles away. He knew, too, with all his soldiering instincts, that the element of surprise when his men were still fresh was vital if they were to stand any chance of driving back Charles and his excited Highlanders. Even though he pressed on his fellow officers the advantages of a surprise attack, Gardiner's advice was not heeded. That evening while the troops relaxed before the planned engagement on the following day, he was seen walking alone in deeply pensive mood.

The night of 20 September 1745 was long and tense. Colonel Gardiner spent it astride his horse, sheltering beside a haystack. At about three in the morning he called for his four domestic attendants, whose task it was to care for him. He dismissed three of them with affectionate admonitions, urging them to care above all things for their eternal destiny. In all probability he spent the next hour in prayer, as was his custom.

Dawn broke over the Firth of Forth to the sound of sickening yells and a furious volley of gunfire. With the advantage of being first to strike, the rebel troops swarmed across the large open field that lay between the two armies. Gardiner and his men charged forward, but almost immediately he received a wound in his chest. Within moments many of his dragoons, who made up the left wing of the army, broke ranks and fled. Wounded, Gardiner fought on, though now dangerously exposed. Another shot hit him on the right thigh. Desperately he tried to rally the remnant of his dragoons for all but a handful had turned back in face of the ferocious onslaught. His faithful attendant, John Foster, begged his master to leave the field before he sustained a fatal wound. But just as Gardiner was considering this option, he noticed a small group of leaderless foot soldiers fighting valiantly nearby. 'Those brave fellows will be cut in pieces for want of a commander,' he cried, riding to their head. 'Fire on, my lads, and fear nothing,' he called out encouragingly.

No sooner had he spoken those words than a Highlander

rode menacingly towards him with a scythe tied to the end of a long pole. He took an aggressive swipe at the Colonel, deeply wounding him in his right arm. Gardiner's sword dropped from his hand. Falling from his horse, he called out to Foster who was still close by, 'Take care of yourself.' Another Highlander, gleeful at the chance to strike at so valued a prize, seeing the wounded man fall, struck him a desperate blow on the head. The last words Gardiner was heard to articulate before losing consciousness were said to have been, 'You are fighting for an earthly crown, I am going to receive a heavenly one.'

The battle was over in five minutes – a rout for King George's forces. Foster ran to a nearby mill, changed his clothes, and disguised as a miller's servant, returned to the battlefield. All was quiet. There he found his much-honoured master, plundered of his watch and boots but still alive. His horse too had been stolen, to be ridden, so it was said, by Prince Charles himself on his march into Derby – an advance that was to mark the end of his triumphs. Lifting his master as carefully as he could onto a cart, Foster carried him across the open fields to the nearby church at Tranent, one that Gardiner knew well. From there he was taken to the minister's house. But by eleven o'clock that morning the trumpeters of heaven had sounded their clarion call of victory for Colonel Gardiner as he passed beyond the pain and noise of battle – faithful unto death.

CHRISTIAN WATT
Not Many Noble

2

A child of eight crept wearily from her bed in a small room built under the stairs in the bank manager's home – a beautiful house overlooking Fraserburgh Bay in north-east Scotland. Here the girl was employed as a maid, and her working day began at five in the morning. First she raked out the fires and then toiled for long hours cleaning the rooms and washing clothes with a scrubbing brush whose bristles had worn to mere stubble. Nor was Christian Watt kindly treated. Addressed by her surname only – a fact she recalled with resentment in later years – Christian was often weak with hunger, and her employer made little allowance for her young age.

The Watt family came from a long-established line of fisher folk living at Broadsea, a wind-buffeted coastal village not more than a mile from Fraserburgh. Poor they might be, but self-respect and family pride ran high; for Christian's family could trace its ancestry back to a certain William Fraser of Philorth – albeit through two illegitimate granddaughters. He in turn was descended from Sir Alexander Fraser himself, who had established Fraserburgh in 1592.

Dried fish and potatoes formed the staple diet for the Watt family, but when spring arrived late, dwindling supplies could mean serious hardship. Christian could remember days when her only meal would consist of half a potato moistened with a little melted lard. Although second to youngest of eight children, the other seven all boys, she too was expected to help towards the family income whenever opportunity arose. So after three months of drudgery at the bank manager's home, the little girl was grateful that her period of employment had finished and she could return home, clutching the three shillings she had earned.

If Christian's day had begun early, her parents had to rise yet earlier. From three in the morning, when her father set off once more to fish the unruly waters of the North Sea, until midnight, they would struggle to provide for the family. Sometimes the girl had seen her parents almost fainting with exhaustion at the end of a day. And despite such toil, with a family of eight to feed, they could scarcely earn enough to lift themselves above subsistence level.

Christian was born in 1833 at 72 Broadsea Main Street, when her mother was already forty-five years of age. Their cottage, a typical Scottish 'butt and ben' cottage, had been the family home for almost two hundred and fifty years. It overlooked the harbour and Christian's seven brothers slept in the 'butt', while her parents were in the 'ben'. Christian's own bed was accommodated in a closet, with a window opening directly onto the sea – that sea, so turbulent and unpredictable, which not only supplied their livelihood but was to bring untold sorrows into their lives.

An attractive and highly intelligent child, Christian quickly learnt to read and write. She also made good progress in punctuation and English grammar and would read every book she could obtain. But Christian's limited education at the little village school was confined to the winter months when fishing was slack, for during the summer months she was needed at home. From the age of eight she was expected to scramble onto the roof of their cottage and lay out the herring to dry in the hot sun. Then she would be fully employed in driving off marauding seagulls which otherwise could rob the family of much of its catch.

But despite the hardships, it was a loving and God-fearing home. A member of the Episcopal church,

Christian's mother taught her children to give thanks to God for his many blessings. When the girl grumbled about her lot, her mother reminded her pointedly that Christ chose fishermen as his first disciples. 'Put on your creel in gratitude to his glory,' she would tell Christian, adding with a touch of family pride, 'Your fathers are grossly superior to these trades people who look down on you.'

When Christian was nine she and her younger brother, Billy, would accompany their mother to the villages and hamlets in the surrounding area, bartering home-cured fish for butter, eggs, milk and cheese. Occasionally they would join their father as he sailed westward around the north coast of Scotland trading his fish for other necessities. By the age of ten, Christian had learnt to gut the herring with her nimble little fingers, working for long hours when the catch was landed. Divided into groups of three, the fish gutters were paid a penny ha'penny for each barrel they filled.

But it was Philorth House, two miles inland from Fraserburgh, home of Alexander Fraser, sixteenth Lord Saltoun, that was to figure most prominently in Christian's mind as she looked back on her childhood days. Here, from the age of ten, she was given intermittent employment as a laundry maid. One of a staff of thirty-nine, Christian was expected to be in the laundry by half past five in the morning. But at least her wages would help provide an extra sack of flour to see her family through the winter months.

For a number of years Christian returned at intervals to work at Philorth and many were the tales she had to tell of her experiences there. Proud, independently-minded and with a huge capacity for indignation, young Christian Watt frequently found herself in trouble. With Lord Saltoun himself often abroad on active army duty, his sister, Mrs Macdowell acted as housekeeper at Philorth. Showing little respect for those who assumed a superior attitude to members of the domestic staff, Christian had a ready answer for any insult, real or imaginary. For years Mrs Macdowell insisted on calling her by her surname only until Christian, with growing self-assurance, could tolerate it no longer. 'They might as well call you Fido or Whiskers,' she commented. 'I think it is the height of impudence and degradation to treat a human being as a dog or cat.' So the next time the lady of the house called out 'Watt!' Christian answered 'Yes, Macdowell!'

Occasionally Lord Saltoun's younger brother William Fraser with his family of twelve would arrive at the old mansion, creating much extra work for the staff. When David, one of William's sons, called at the laundry one day, he said in a particularly snooty voice, 'Ask Fairy Kitta to collect the laundry.' Inflamed at being addressed in such an insulting way, Christian snapped back, 'Look, Slavie Davie, you are lucky I did not make your lugs dirl! [ears sting].' But her vengeance was not yet complete:

The next morning David Fraser was all toffed up to go out shooting. I had a pile of sheets in my hand, hidden among them was a decanter of scent . . . I pretended to stumble and sent the whole contents over him in front of all his brother officers. I said, 'Now you are *Fairy Fraser*.' He stank all day, and they all ragged him.[1]

Possibly delighted at seeing his brother embarrassed, Murray Fraser, another of William's sons, frequently made his way to the laundry, where Christian, by now an attractive and vivacious girl in her late teens, could be found. No errand appeared too trivial to bring the young man there, until the head of the laundry staff playfully offered him a job. But even Christian was taken aback when Murray asked if he could come home with her one Saturday night, as he wished to ask Christian's father for permission to marry his daughter. Far from being flattered by the

[1] Quotations from Christian Watt's writings reprinted by permission of the Peters Fraser & Dunlop Group Ltd.

attentions of one in a station in life so much superior to her own, Christian, still a stranger to the humbling grace of God, commented. 'I was horrified. Not that I thought these people better than myself – save my Lord and Saviour, I can see none better but plenty of people worse!' Christian's father resolved the predicament by refusing his permission until his daughter had come of age; and by that time Murray Fraser was on active army life in India.

When Christian Watt was twenty-one tragedy struck the family, not once, but five times over. In the spring of 1854 a ship on which two of her older brothers were sailing as crew members foundered off the coast of New Jersey, with all 250 passengers and the entire crew lost. Another brother, James, died after contracting a rare blood condition in Australia that August. Meanwhile Christian's younger brother, Billy, and another brother, Jock, were serving in the Navy during the Crimean War. Both perished in November 1854, when their ship was sabotaged in the Black Sea and blew up after hitting a reef. In six short months the family was reduced from eight to three; Sandy, Christian's eldest brother, had been twenty-nine, and Billy was only eighteen.

Christian was devastated. Knowing nothing but formal religion, she had no place of refuge in her grief. She witnessed her parents grow old, as it were, overnight. For a year she could not bring herself to go into her brothers' bedroom or touch their possessions. But wishing to save her mother the anguish of such a task, Christian plucked up courage at last and tidied the forlorn little room. Her other two brothers were both abroad, 'so I had to carry the whole burden of a broken world. I did not think I would ever smile again. My father never spoke of his sons, even years after, but it brought a lump to his throat,' wrote Christian many years later.

When Christian learnt that Sandy had made her the sole

beneficiary of his will, she could hardly bring herself to touch the money – a sum, considerable for those days, of nearly £300. But after two years she was persuaded to travel to New York, where it was banked, and claim it. A cousin, captain of a sailing vessel, offered to take Christian there and collect her again on his return journey eight months later. Those colourful months were among the happiest of Christian's life. Engaged as a table maid to a Mrs Jerome – later to become grandmother to Sir Winston Churchill – Christian met a wide circle of celebrities as the Jeromes threw expensive dinner parties for their associates. Her wages were four times greater than anything she could have earned at home. Mr Jerome undertook to trace Christian's legacy, and with his influential backing she obtained it within a week.

These were the days immediately prior to the American Civil War. Emotions ran high in New York, and Christian herself, coming from a downtrodden community, burned with indignation for the underprivileged:

In America I had come face to face with reality, and the bitterness that burns in coloured folks' hearts towards those who brought them there; the African chiefs who sold their own people for gold are equally as guilty as the purchasers. As a subjugated Scot I could sympathise, for a handful of greedy blockhead peers should never have had the power to vote to sell an independent minded nation for English gold.

Back in Broadsea once more, Christian was forcefully reminded of the sorrows of her stricken parents, who refused to touch any of Sandy's inheritance, insisting that Christian herself would need it all. But they were anxious that their daughter, tall, attractive and now twenty-five years of age, should consider marriage. But whom could she marry, wondered Christian, for the thought of marrying a fisherman appalled the young woman, who had already tasted too much of the hardships which such a life could bring. When Christian first set eyes on 'Jimmy Brave', however, she sensed, despite her own disinclinations, that this man would eventually be her husband.

James Sim had gained his nickname at the age of eighteen when he swam alone amidst tempestuous waves to attach a rope onto a sinking vessel. All the crew of the Norwegian ship were rescued, and James was presented with a gold watch as a mark of gratitude. Two years Christian's senior, he had attended the same school and church as she, though they had never spoken before. Tall, intelligent, and with wide-ranging interests, he had also served in the Navy during the Crimean War and, like Christian, came from a fishing family, though from the nearby village of Pitullie.

In January 1859 Christian and James Sim were formally engaged – with a legally binding contract drawn up by a lawyer, as the custom was. Three months later James was due to sail for Greenland on a whaling vessel and would be gone for at least six months. Fraught with dangers, such an expedition invariable took a heavy toll on the lives of the crew. Girls knew well that when they waved good-bye to their men, it might easily be the last time they would see them.

Two weeks before the ships were to sail, Christian's mother became ill and was taken to hospital in Aberdeen. Her father accompanied her, leaving Christian on her own in Broadsea. Alone in the house one stormy evening, with the wind outside whipping the waves to a fury, Christian's mind was also in turmoil. She poked the peats on the fire to a blaze and sat gazing into the flames. Did she really want to marry at all? She hardly knew. Did she love James enough? He could be harsh – even cruel and demanding at times . . .

Then came heavy steps approaching the cottage. James himself had called to see her. Late into the night they sat talking as the peats on the fire died to embers. By now the rain was lashing down on the window panes, and the weather had become so wild that Christian suggested that James slept in the butt end of the cottage. But the temptation of being alone with Christian proved too great for the young man. He left his bed in the far end of the cottage and joined Christian in hers.

By four the next morning, Christian, ashamed and troubled at what had happened, urged James to crawl out through the back window, lest any of the ever-watchful neighbours should see him go. Before he left her, James pleaded with Christian that they should marry prior to his departure for Greenland. But Christian was still unsure. Only after he had sailed did she realise she was expecting a child.

To become pregnant before marriage was not considered a serious offence in the church to which Christian belonged; but to give birth to a child out of wedlock was a misdemeanour of much greater consequence and would involve discipline before the Kirk Session. If James returned in November, as he hoped, they could marry and nothing would be said. Christian's child, however, was due in January, and she knew well that arctic conditions could easily prevent the fleet returning on time. With her rebellious nature, her hatred of hypocrisy and her capacity for indignation, Christian's mind was filled with angry thoughts and vindictive plans as she contemplated the discipline that might await her:

During the conflict between Episcopalians and Presbyterians several times my ancestors had wrecked the church; now I would wreck the session. I would ask to appear in the body of the kirk not the vestry, and I would start on one elder, a Fraserburgh business man, who in the past had been known to frequent bawdy houses in Aberdeen. In fact I toyed with the idea of turning down the father and keeping the child – today I wish I had made that decision.

Christian was in deep trouble. But at last God's time to

intervene in the life of this independent and strong-minded young woman had come. As the months crept by, she grew more and more anxious. She began to seek God earnestly. Her experience is best told in her own words:

During the weeks of waiting, I read nothing but the Bible, and to my own joy and astonishment I found the Lord Jesus as my own personal Saviour. Only in my own personal experience did I discover how man was alienated from God, and how we were reconciled by his death on Calvary's cross. In my own room that night I knew I had passed from death unto life.

> *Oh joyous hour when God to me*
> *A vision gave of Calvary,*
> *My bonds were loosed, my soul unbound,*
> *I stand upon redemption ground.*

Now Christian knew that she must marry James, and though the years stretching before her might be filled with privations and difficulties, nothing could separate her from the love of Christ.

James returned safely from the whaling in the last week of November, and he and Christian were married a few days later, standing in the middle of the floor of the tiny cottage at 72 Broadsea. They lived together with Christian's parents occupying the butt end of the cottage until January when their son, whom they also called James, was born. After this they moved across to Pitullie to share a house with James' aunt. Christian's immediate priority was to buy a boat for her new husband so that he could be self-employed. Most of her legacy money was devoted to this expensive project, which made it impossible for the young couple to afford a home of their own. So when Christian's second child, Peter, was born and more space became a pressing need, the family moved in with James' mother.

A serious mistake, this move brought continual tension and distress into Christian's life. Her mother-in-law, a dominant woman, felt that her place in her son's affections had been usurped. She criticised Christian mercilessly. Christian's own inflammable temperament, exacerbated by the limited space in the home, brought many clashes between the two women – a severe test of Christian's new-found faith. Added to this, business was poor. Fish were not so plentiful in the seas around Pitullie, and limited by her two small boys, Christian was not able to walk into Fraserburgh to buy extra fish to cure and sell. In her spare moments, however, she found consolation from the pages of Scripture and gained strength for her efforts to please her mother-in-law.

Not long after this Christian's own mother died. A true believer, she had struggled all her life against poverty and crushing sorrows. Now in her dying she cast herself once more on the mercy and pity of the Son of God. 'Give me your hand', she said to her daughter who was alone caring for her back in the family cottage in Broadsea. As Christian clasped her hand, her mother spoke clearly:

> *Jesus my heart's dear refuge,*
> *Jesus has died for me,*
> *Safe on the Rock of Ages,*
> *Ever my trust shall be.*

When Christian's father entered the room she referred once more to the sons they had lost. And then her hard life was finished. Christian felt the death of her mother deeply. She would have liked to move back to Broadsea to care for her elderly father, but her husband firmly opposed the idea. So she found rented accommodation for him in Sandhaven, a village adjacent to Broadsea.

For several more years Christian and James lived with his mother in Pitullie. The family grew as two more boys, George and Joseph, were born. But James was hard on his sons. An upright and disciplined man himself, he expected high standards from the boys; and often his two oldest,

James and Peter, who had a good measure of their mother's flair, would rush from the house in terror to avoid the severe beatings their father would administer for relatively minor offences. 'Christ never drives folks,' Christian would protest, 'he leads. You are doing the boys no good by thrashing them so much.'

Nor did Christian's relationship with her mother-in-law improve. Despite her high-sounding religious language, the younger woman discovered that her mother-in-law knew no true heart religion. In common with many other church-goers of that time, much of her religious profession was a facade. Christian commented wryly:

One thing I have learnt in this world, 60 percent of folk who call themselves Christians are fakes, especially around North East Scotland and the Moray Forth seaboard . . . I have beheld the saints on a Sunday night forming little groups in parting at their kirk doors with that 'holier than thou' kind of tone of voice. They are either discussing herring or harvest or houses, but not the Lord Jesus who had not place to lay his head. My mother-in-law was a typical example.

Year by year the tensions and misunderstanding increased, though Christian fully recognised that her explosive nature also made her a problem to her mother-in-law. But constant and unnecessary criticisms gradually wore away Christian's patience until at last she could stand it no longer. On occasions the Congregational minister came to have tea with James' mother. The delicious smell of fresh baked gingerbread wafted through the house, the best crockery was brought out . . .

And into the middle of one tea party stormed Christian, angry and distressed. She blurted out her tale of long-repressed hurt and heaped-up indignities that she had suffered at her mother-in-law's hand over the years. 'Jinna (her mother-in-law) was dumbstruck and his reverence flummoxed,' reported Christian. But Jinna was not dumbstruck for long. Her reprisal was sharp and cruel and revealed why Christian, despite all her efforts, had been quite unable to please her.

She told him she had advised her son not to have anything to do with me. I was grossly mismatched, I did not share his interests; but her chief objection was a history of insanity and consumption in our family; and that our marriage could never be a success.

Such injustice stung Christian, who realised that her outburst had been wrong; but, she added, 'only matchless grace kept my hands off her.' The accusation of insanity in the family rankled deeply, and would cause Christian untold pain in the years to come. Now she knew she could no longer stay in that home. 'I took my troubles to the throne of grace to be resolved,' she wrote. With the remainder of her legacy and with her father's help she managed to scrape together enough money to buy a plot of land in Sandhaven, where her father lived. There a two-storied house was built in which the family could occupy while letting the upper rooms to finance the project.

After only seven months at Sandhaven Christian's father died. In her heart she longed to go back to Broadsea, but again James would not consider it. Three more children were born in rapid succession: in 1867 twins, Isabella and Andrew, and the following year another daughter, Nellie. Christian, now thirty-four, did her best to augment her husband's meagre income by gutting and curing herring as well as caring for seven children all under the age of nine.

At last in 1870 the tenants in Christian's family home in Broadsea unexpectedly moved out. James was far away on a fishing expedition. Seizing her opportunity, Christian, whose nervous health was threatening to give way under the stress of her circumstances, moved the whole family back to Broadsea. The boys helped her pile their possessions on carts, and 'in no time the butt and ben lums [chimneys] were reeking and I was happy.' When James returned he discovered his family safely installed in 72 Broadsea, with the Sandhaven home mortgaged to a new owner. Christian reports, 'My husband was furious,' but clearly he soon forgave his unpredictable wife for she continues, 'we had seven years of happiness and great sadness.' Here three more children were born: Watt, Mary and lastly Charlotte.

Life had never been easy, but now the effects of the Industrial Revolution were felt even among the fishing communities of north east Scotland. With fish curing becoming big business, the fishermen's wives were scarcely able to sell their own cured fish in exchange for other commodities. But eleven-year-old Peter, Christian and James' second son, a mischievous and likeable lad, would often bring home additional items for his family since he too had started work. After the family had moved from Pitullie relations with her mother-in-law began to improve. Christian regularly took her children across to see their grandmother, and she became genuinely fond of them, but especially of Peter.

This boy had always had a passion for the sea. As a small child he would paddle around the shore in an old wooden tub, until he became known as 'Peter the Rover'. His dream was fulfilled as he took his first job on a vessel carrying herring to the Baltic. After this he sailed to a number of places with cargoes of herring. In 1874 thirteen-year-old Peter sailed for Prussia. But one morning as Christian was busy cooking the family meal she suddenly and distinctly heard Peter's voice calling out for her. By that strange bond that links hearts closely joined in love, she knew her boy was dying and was crying out for his mother. James, equally distressed, did all he could to discover what had happened to his son. Some months later he learnt that Peter had drowned, but no-one seemed to know exactly how. The captain of the vessel reported that he was buried in Kronigsburg, and brought home the eight shillings the lad had earned – money Christian could never spend, but donated to a children's hospital in Aberdeen.

Peter's death brought a new tenderness to his father. No longer did he chastise his sons harshly, and he went out of his way to be kinder to Christian. But it also marked a deterioration in Christian's nervous health. Two years later a further sorrow struck the family when Joseph, their fourth son, who was then eleven, died of tetanus after bathing a wound in water from the cattle's drinking trough. Christian wrote sadly, 'I nursed him three days. It was heart rending to see the sick child in convulsions. "The Lord giveth and the Lord taketh away. Blessed be the name of the Lord."' The cost of the funeral rocked the family's precarious finances, and they were forced to mortgage the boat until they could save enough to buy it back.

1877 had been a good year for Broadsea fishermen. But in August, just three years after Peter's death, Christian was plunged once more into deep grief. James and his two remaining older sons were out on the boat, preparing to sail west. Christian had been washing the blankets in readiness for the trip. Suddenly the sky blackened as storm clouds swept in from the sea; and as Christian hurried to rescue her washing from the impending rain, the wind tossed the waves so high that they seemed to rise above her like rolling hills. Just at that moment she caught a glimpse of their own boat riding high on the crest of the turbulent waves around Kinnairds Head. All was not well with it – instinct told her that.

A knock on her door some hours later hardly surprised her. The Congregational minister had called. 'Which one of my folk is lost?' asked Christian despairingly. 'It's the husband,' was his simple reply. James had been washed overboard as he struggled to secure the rigging against the storm. Clad in heavy fisherman's garments and leather boots with iron heels, he had nevertheless swum to a nearby boat, but as he was about to hoist himself up a huge breaker crashed against him sweeping him away. Perhaps it had caused concussion, for he would have been thrown against the side of the boat – but this she would never know. It was a blow Christian could hardly face. She had loved James, despite all their differences. 'I could only say to God, "I was dumb, because thou didst it."' Now she must fend on her own and provide for her eight children.

To know her husband had been drowned so near to home and yet be unable even to bury him was a burden Christian found hard to bear. Forlornly she scoured the nearby beaches in case his body had been washed ashore. But God, the Protector of the fatherless and the widow, drew near to Christian in her fruitless search. As she crossed the sands not far from her home, she felt him come to her in an experience she could only describe as 'a baptism with the Holy Ghost and fire'. Now she knew that God loved her still – a desolate widow – and still had a purpose for her life. As she reached home she felt a new sense of peace in her soul, assuring her that all would be well, whatever the hardships.

Christian's oldest son, James, soon went to sea, but she still had seven children to feed and clothe. She owned her boat, she owned her house – for this she was grateful. But she had little income and had to employ a man to skipper the boat. 'I was sick with worry, neither eating nor sleeping'. With the little income remaining she bought as much fish as she could from the Fraserburgh market, but it was not sufficient to exchange for the food the family needed. Often she would hunt the beaches for small shell-fish which she could take home and cook for the children as they returned hungry from school. Sometimes when baby Charlotte was asleep, she would throw her arms around Ranger, the old family dog, and weep uncontrollably. Looking back on her life she was to write:

There is a time to laugh and a time to weep, a time to mourn and a time to dance. These were the second great tears of my life. How I missed my mother, who had also known grief. Both my parents are safe within the veil of salvation, but how I wished I still had them when I lost my man. I had my trust in Christ, the Man of Sorrows, and knew what he felt as he stood before Pontius Pilate, knowing full well he must go to Calvary to die and rise again to redeem mankind from sin.

Christian's doctor realised that she must have a break from the stress and suggested that she should go to the Aberdeen mental hospital for a complete rest. Christian hesitated. Who would care for the family? Apart from thirteen-year-old George, she had six children under the age of eleven, with Charlotte, the youngest, not yet two. But as her depression deepened Christian knew she had no option. Her cousin said she would keep an eye on the children, but all the day-to-day running of the home – cooking, cleaning, washing and checking that the other children went to school neatly dressed, fell to ten-year-old Isabella.

Cornhill, the mental hospital on the outskirts of Aberdeen, was scarcely the place for one suffering nervous collapse. Noticing that all the doors were locked behind her as she entered, Christian felt a prisoner – far from home. With her natural self-esteem and pride, she could not bring herself to join the other patients in the dining room and watch the way they tackled their meals. Later she was to take a more philosophical view, but for the present, she was allowed a job in the kitchen, and there she also ate her meals. Despite the locked doors, a kindly, enlightened and understanding regime prevailed at Cornhill, with the hospital staff genuinely dedicated to the welfare of the patients. There Christian stayed over the winter months of 1877.

Delight filled her heart as spring came round once more, with new life bursting from bud and branch; and especially when Christian was told that she was considered well enough to be discharged. Reunited with the family, she found the home spotlessly clean and everything under control. Isabella had managed with admirable efficiency.

But a shock awaited her. She discovered that to have been a patient in a mental institution brought with it an undisguised contempt from erstwhile friends and neighbours. For a woman so highly intelligent as Christian Watt, this was hard indeed to bear.

Being in an asylum is a terrible stigma. It should not be, for the same hand who put it upon me can put it upon anybody. Mental illness should not be confused with mental deficiency. They are whole worlds apart, but equally sad. When I came home I found folk constantly trying to shun me as if I had leprosy. The usual pattern was to smile and be pleasant for a moment, then make some sort of excuse that they were in an awful hurry to do something. I went to farms in the country, and many places where they could see me coming I found the door barred in my face. It was a terrifying experience. I had only Christ who dined with publicans and sinners and who is a real friend to social outcasts.

Christian pressed on, trying to sell her fish. But everywhere the response was the same. No-one wanted to buy from her. At the end of a day she would return home with a basket as heavy as when she set out, and her heart even heavier. At one country mansion where she had often sold her fish in the past, she overheard the lady of the house instructing the housekeeper to send Christian away. 'Under no circumstances give her tea or anything that might encourage her. We can't have a mad woman coming about the place.' Christian resisted her strong urge to go in and hit the speaker.

That winter the family nearly starved. Not everyone ignored Christian and she soon learnt who her true friends were, but she grew steadily weaker. At last one day, she fainted, nearly falling into the fire. Again the doctor said she must go back to Cornhill for a rest. This time Christian gladly agreed, for it was a haven of peace for her troubled mind. Isabella once more cared for the family.

During the three years after her first admittance to Cornhill, Christian spent most of her time with her family, only going back to the hospital for periods of rest when the tension and anxiety became too intense for her broken spirit. Few others, however, cared to be seen associating with her. She managed to secure a job splitting and gutting fish – a task that was almost second nature to her. Then she overheard a woman say to her employer, 'I think it is very wrong that a woman out of the asylum should be working with knives.' She lost her job immediately. With no other means of feeding her growing family, Christian was reduced to gathering whelks from the shore left by the receding tide. Here at least she had an advantage, for no-one would come within a quarter of a mile of her on either side, so she was able to fill her basket quickly with the best of the shellfish. Sadly Christian recollected the black population of New York, whose plight had kindled her sympathies so many years ago. One option suggested itself to her – she would emigrate with her entire family to America. At least there she could start afresh.

On a bitter winter's day in 1879, with hands numbed by the cold, Christian broke the ice on the rock pools and gathered shellfish. Arriving home so cold she could hardly carry the pail, she found a letter awaiting her from the consulate to whom she had applied for emigration papers. Opening it quickly, she read that her application had been rejected because of her medical record. Her spirits plummeted. The final door of hope had been slammed in her face.

Christian's eyes lit on her small hen house with its half a dozen birds. They were not laying, for like Christian and her children, they were inadequately fed. With that Christian's mind snapped. 'It was as distinct as a butter plate breaking on the floor,' she recalled. Seizing a bottle of paraffin, she poured it over the hen house, intending to set it alight. Her son George, now fourteen, struggled with his mother to prevent her doing such a crazy thing.

The next day Christian was certified insane. A cab drew up to the house, and though the children clung frantically to their mother, she was removed forcibly and taken to Cornhill for ever. The home at 72 Broadsea and all the family's personal possessions were to be put up for public auction to pay for Christian's accommodation. The children were to be split up. The three youngest, Watt, Mary and Charlotte were assigned to an orphanage, until the offer of a kind friend to care for them prevented them from being taken there. Nellie, who was ten, was employed as a maid in one of the nearby country houses; Andrew, now twelve, also took employment and was cared for by friends; and his twin, Isabella left the area and went to Lowestoft to work in the fish industry. The dog, Ranger, was shot, despite the tears of the children, who buried him themselves on the brae.

Only George, too old for an orphanage, had nowhere to go. He had the task of finally locking up the family home at 72 Broadsea and handing the key to the commissioners. A few nights later fierce storms raged across the north of Scotland, causing widespread damage. Half the roof of number 72 was ripped off and blown into the sea. A local man, hurrying home to shelter from the elements, suddenly noticed movements under an upturned boat.

It was George – he had no other accommodation. This kindly man and his wife provided a home for the boy until George married.

In all these intense trials and sorrows of Christian's life, her faith still shone out steadily and brightly. How must the trumpeters of heaven have sounded out their notes of triumph as this much-afflicted believer was able to write with unwavering confidence:

I knew my landing in the Asylum was all part of my fiery trials. It is the refining pot for silver and the furnace for gold. Job is our finest example. 'He knoweth the way that I take. When he has tried me he will bring me forth as gold'; or as the silversmith who purifies until he can see his own image. I have had the experience of both the refining pot and the furnace of affliction . . . and no matter how fierce, I will eventually come forth unhurt.

The remainder of Christian's long life, for she lived until the age of ninety, must be quickly told. With adequate food and rest she soon regained her mental stability, but never again was she able to go home. Far from spending her days in regrets and self-pity, she soon became her active self. Three days a week she went to the Aberdeen fish market, buying and gutting fish, saving every penny she could for, she hoped to buy back her home one day. She worked in the hospital kitchens and in the laundry, endearing herself to the staff. But all the time Christian had a yet higher motive:

I got to know the trawl skippers and their wives and all the shore porters . . . and I spoke to them all of their never-dying souls. I worked very hard and sewed by hand dozens of patchwork quilts and I did a lot of embroidery for the Aberdeen shops.

And as new patients came into Cornhill, many like Christian herself only suffering from nervous exhaustion, she would seek them out, console and encourage them, always speaking to them of the Man of Sorrows who was acquainted with grief.

She worried about her children. When ten-year-old Watt died of scarlettina, Christian was allowed home to the funeral. She grieved deeply for the child's short sad life, but also had to admit an element of relief. 'My son Watt was free from the cares of a loveless upbringing. Thy will be done,' she wrote. His death brought back her depression, however, and she was confined to bed for a fortnight.

The rent from the boat which Christian and James had owned paid for the care of the remaining two children, Mary and Charlotte, until they could be self-supporting. Although there was no hope of Christian being discharged, Isabella would occasionally return from Lowestoft when business was slack and rent a cottage where her mother and the three younger girls, Nellie, Mary and Charlotte, could be together at week-ends. George married at a young age, but Andrew, clearly suffering from his disturbed childhood, became a heavy drinker.

James, Christian's eldest son, also caused his mother much anxiety as he cast aside her faith, adopting a reactionary agnosticism. To have seen all his mother's possessions auctioned for a fraction of their worth had embittered the young man. Christian gave herself to prayer for him; but his self-righteous and godless attitudes only seemed to harden. When he wanted to dispense with a Christian ceremony at his marriage because, as he told his mother, he did not wish to be a hypocrite, Christian was illogically averse, regarding the marriage as invalid. But God heard her prayers for James, and ten years later both he and his wife were converted through the preaching of a Faith missioner in Stornaway.

When James had saved enough money to buy a boat of his own he called it Venture. When his mother asked him why he had chosen that name, he replied:

My soul is now united
With Christ the living vine;
For long his grace I slighted,
But now I call him mine.
Soon as my soul I ventured
On the atoning blood,
The Holy Spirit entered
And I was born of God.

Set against this consolation, Christian faced further adversity over her daughter Nellie. When the girl told her mother that she hoped soon to marry a young man whose child she was expecting, Christian must have recollected her own early life. But shortly before they were due to marry, the man discovered that Nellie's mother was in a mental institution, and refused to marry her. Nellie's distress was acute, and not long after her child was still-born, Nellie herself dying only a few days later. Christian's indignation and grief again brought back her depression. But, as she commented wryly, 'the mills of God grind slowly,' for many years later the woman this man eventually married came into Cornhill suffering from a mental affliction. Grace triumphed over nature in Christian's fiery temperament as she was able to speak kindly to the troubled woman and rejoice at her recovery.

The years passed quickly and not unhappily for Christian as her children and then her grandchildren would come to visit her. A new doctor, was appointed to take overall charge of Cornhill Dr Reid appreciated Christian's unusual capabilities and worth, often consulting her about patients who were admitted. He encouraged her to write down all she could remember of her life experiences, and soon sheet after sheet of memoirs came from Christian's ready pencil – for pens were forbidden at Cornhill. Her accuracy of recollection, her choice of words and sharp insights demonstrated her exceptional intelligence.[1]

Christian lived on through the years of the First World War, two more of her daughters dying before she did: Isabella at fifty-four and Charlotte in the great 'flu epidemic after the war. A number of her grandsons served in the armed forces, and Christian followed all dispatches from the front with avid interest. As young men were admitted to hospital suffering from shell-shock she would sit with them and speak of the hope of the gospel as they were able to comprehend it.

James at last fulfilled his life ambition and with his mother's help bought back 72 Broadsea. After his wife died he begged his mother to come and live there with him, but the memories were too painful for her. And so in 1923 Christian's long life of suffering and service for her God came to an end. She did not fear to die: 'I look forward to passing through the valley of the shadow of death, but I will not pass through death itself, for I feel in eternity I shall learn more and more about God,' wrote Christian in extreme old age. Conscious to the last, she told her three sons who were at her bedside that she was happy and was going into the presence of the Lord.

Often scorned, often destitute, Christian Watt demonstrates through her story – a story which she herself related so lucidly and dramatically in her declining years, that God indeed delights to choose for his own those whom this world may disdain; for 'not many wise, not many noble are called. But God has chosen the weak things of the world, to put to shame the things that are mighty . . . The things which are despised God has chosen . . . that no flesh should glory in his presence.'

---

[1] Published as *The Christian Watt Papers*, edited and with an introduction by General Sir David Fraser, (Caledonian Books, 1988). These papers contain a full account of Christian Watt's life.

ARCHIBALD BROWN
Forgotten Preacher

3

Wedged in among the crowds that thronged the Surrey Gardens Music Hall to hear the preaching of Charles Haddon Spurgeon stood a boy of twelve. 'Go home to your friends and tell them how great things the Lord has done for you' was the text on which the twenty-two-year-old preacher based his sermon. The boy in the crowd never forgot the message he heard that morning. Over forty years later Archibald Brown was to write, 'I can still remember the desire that sprang up in my heart to tell so good a story' – a desire that was to be remarkably fulfilled.

But Archibald Geikie Brown's early years were far from promising in spite of the outstanding men among his forebears. His paternal grandfather, David Brown, close friend of William Wilberforce and member of the 'Clapham Sect', had been nicknamed 'Bible Brown' for his absorbing interest in the formation of the British and Foreign Bible Society. His mother, Emma, was the daughter of Job Heath, 'the fourth' – for four successive generations the name had been passed from father to son, each 'Job Heath' being a man of strong Christian character. Archibald's grandfather was the last of this remarkable line. The family had played a significant role among the Dissenters since the first Job Heath was baptised as a believer in 1711. Known for his prayerfulness, it was written of Job Heath the fourth: 'As the flower seeks the sun and the bird its evening nest, so did his soul seek the mercy seat. He was at home there. Not only was prayer his element and his recreation, it was his business, and he looked for results as a matter of course.' We may be sure that when Job Heath heard of the birth of his new grandson, Archibald, in July 1844, he followed the child's progress with his continual prayers.

Like many other boys, Archibald Brown seemed to have an inbuilt antipathy to the necessary disciplines of education. Athletic in build and fun-loving by nature, he confessed that during his school days he was 'more distinguished for larking than for learning'. Nor did he respond to the challenges of the gospel, though he regularly heard the impassioned appeals of C.H. Spurgeon at New Park Street Chapel, where his father served as a deacon. Later he was to recall another sermon he had heard from the young preacher, also in the Surrey Gardens Music Hall, but two years after the previous occasion:

The sermon that most impressed me spiritually was from the text, 'Compel them to come in.' Were the Music Hall now standing I could pick out the seat I occupied just behind the pulpit. How did he labour to save us! His pleading was pathetic [full of pathos]. I had a feeling that if he went on much longer, I should be bound to be converted . . . I believe a multitude *was* saved that morning, though a lad of fourteen was not among the number.

In view of his son's aversion to study, Archibald Brown's father decided to make the financial sacrifice necessary to send the boy to a highly regarded boarding school in Brighton. Here, under the watchful eyes of his tutors, Archibald would be forced to attend to his academic work. For two or three years the boy was prevailed upon to comply with regulations, but when he was fifteen he absconded from school, arriving back at his home in London when he was least expected.

Realising the futility of trying to co-erce the boy into continuing his education, Archibald's father apprenticed him to a tea-broker in the City, hoping Archibald might eventually make his fortune in the tea trade in China. But the erratic youth found his new occupation equally dull. His attention was elsewhere, for his eyes had alighted on an attractive young woman, Annie Biggs, a girl of marked godliness of life. Her influence on Archibald Brown was to be profound.

As the friendship between Archibald and Annie developed she found opportunities to influence the young man for good. Hearing that a well-known speaker, Captain Arthur Blackwood was holding regular gatherings in his own home in Streatham, Annie invited her friend to accompany her to hear him speak.

God's time had now come for Archibald Brown. Whereas he had previously managed to silence the clamour of a disturbed conscience, he found he could do so no longer. The message he heard searched him out and demanded a response. For two days and nights he wrestled with its implications, crying out to the God of mercy to save his soul.

Those days of spiritual anguish were to be forever etched on his memory; he could even recall the exact spot where the final transaction of grace took place – under an oak tree near his home. Now he knew and felt his sins forgiven. Overcome with relief and delight, the exuberant young man threw his cap high up into the branches of the tree. In future years he loved to recall the occasion: 'I remember what God did for me forty-seven years ago,' he would say. 'In a moment he arrested a careless young man who was cursing and swearing on Monday, and singing God's praises at twelve o'clock on Wednesday, and has been singing them ever since.' He would also add that his first act as a Christian was to climb the oak tree to rescue his cap!

Without delay Archibald Brown visited Captain Blackwood to tell him of God's dealings with him. To his amazement, the Captain conducted the new convert down to the railway sidings where some men were laying a new line. 'This young man will come every morning to read the Scriptures to you,' announced the Captain. There was no escape. The exercise and discipline involved in complying with such an injunction steadied and confirmed Brown in his new-found faith.

Not long after this a London City Missioner invited the sixteen-year-old to accompany him to a meeting one evening to read 'the lesson'. But discovering that he was expected to read extracts from *The Pilgrim's Progress* rather than the Scriptures and that there would be no preaching, the youth protested in astonishment, 'Is that all you are going to give the people?'

'Don't you think that will do them good?' rejoined the missioner.

'It might,' replied Brown, 'but there should be preaching – preaching Christ.'

'If you think so,' replied the missioner good-naturedly, 'you'd better preach.'

'I've never done such a thing before, but I'll try,' came the young man's ready answer.

Glancing around at the gathering of twenty elderly ladies in a hall that could accommodate a hundred and fifty, Archibald declared that he would first go and find a congregation. Calling around to several of the local public houses, he persuaded the customers to come and hear him preach. 'I have never preached before,' he told them, 'but tonight I am going to have a try.' With a cheery toast to the young man with sufficient cheek to expect them to abandon their favourite pastime in favour of a sermon, thirty or forty men left their glasses and made their way to the nearby hall. When his 'congregation' had assembled Brown preached an impromptu, but effective sermon on 'Thou shalt call his name Jesus.'

After so unconventional a start, Archibald Brown was soon looking around for further opportunities to serve his God. Applying to the Sunday School superintendent, he asked if he might teach a class. With a reputation for fooling around and a known genius for mimicry, Archibald found his offer was received with coolness and suspicion. The youth must have an ulterior motive. Perhaps he wished to disrupt proceedings and delight his friends with his theatrics. So the senior man firmly rejected Brown's offer. No class was available, nor was there need for any additional Sunday School staff. Unwilling to be turned away so peremptorily, Brown persisted, 'But may I teach here if I bring my own class?'

'If you bring your own class, I cannot keep you out,' replied the other. During the following week, young Archibald Brown could be seen knocking at hundreds of doors, often in the most deprived areas of the neighbourhood, and posing the same question: 'Have you any children who do not go to Sunday School?' To the superintendent's amazement, Brown arrived the following Sunday, followed by thirty or more youths, many older than himself. So began a young men's Bible Class which would be significantly used by God in the years that were to come. Doubtless Annie, whose affections Brown still eagerly courted, would have been a highly interested spectator of all these events.

In spite of his zeal, however, Archibald Brown, like many young believers, knew times of doubt and fear lest his professions should be hollow and his sense of forgiveness imaginary. As with the oak tree of his conversion experience, Brown could point to the exact spot where he was standing when God gave him an added assurance of his love and forgiveness. Carrying a bag of tea samples, Brown was crossing Mincing Lane when a verse of Scripture flashed forcibly across his mind: 'The just shall live by faith.' So dramatically did the implications of this truth dawn on him that he stood rooted to the spot and only narrowly escaped being knocked to the ground by a passing cab.

With new assurance Archibald Brown applied to C.H. Spurgeon for baptism. In 1861, shortly before his seventeenth birthday, he was baptised in the Metropolitan Tabernacle – opened only three months earlier. Brown was among the first of over 14,000 to be baptised in that building before Spurgeon's death in 1892. He did not join the Tabernacle membership, but became instead a member of a Congregational church near his home in Brixton. Perhaps he felt he could be of more service to God in his own locality. And so it proved, for within weeks he was asked to address a Saturday evening prayer meeting – an engagement that rapidly became a permanent fixture.

Requests for the young man to preach multiplied and soon he found himself called upon almost every evening. Life as a trainee tea broker, and even time spent with Annie, ran a definite second to Archibald Brown's all-absorbing interest. His father, who had invested heavily in his son's training, was not pleased with the turn events. A natural pessimist, he seemed blind to his son's gifts and expressed his disapproval. A tolerable tea-trader his son might well make if only he would apply himself to his work; but any aspirations he might have to be a preacher of the gospel were out of the question in his view. Archibald Brown's father shared his dismay with his pastor and his fellow deacons at the Tabernacle, but, not unexpectedly, received little sympathy from them.

At last Archibald knew that he must resolve the situation and decide between his increasing commitment to Christian service and his employment as a tea-trader. So when Spurgeon heard a knock on his vestry door after a midweek service in the summer of 1862 he was not surprised to discover Archibald Brown waiting to speak to him. 'I have heard all about you from your father,' declared Spurgeon, 'I have been expecting you. Come in.' Brown's heart must have sunk at such a greeting but to his delight the great preacher readily accepted the eager young man and offered him a place at his Pastor's College.

In November 1862, when Archibald Brown was still only eighteen years of age, Spurgeon assigned him to his first pastorate, a group of twenty people meeting in a hotel lounge in Bromley, Kent. With characteristic zeal, Brown began not only to preach but also to discharge all the practical duties connected with the work: opening doors, dusting furniture, laying out and gathering in hymnbooks. On the first Sunday twenty gathered to hear him preach, but after three weeks the number had dwindled to sixteen. Cast into the depths by this apparent rejection of his efforts, Brown declared that if numbers fell any lower he would give up, or else there would be no one to accept his resignation.

But gradually numbers climbed again. Soon there were twenty, and each week witnessed a gradual increase. After two years several hundred attended regularly and the church clearly needed to erect a building of its own. In July 1864 the foundation stone of the present-day Bromley Baptist Church was laid by C.H. Spurgeon. Job Heath the Fourth wrote a characteristic note to his grandson on the occasion:

In case anything should prevent me being present at Bromley to witness the laying of the corner stone for the chapel – where I trust you may be honoured by our adorable Redeemer in bringing many out of darkness into the glorious light of the gospel for many years to come – I wish to say I will give £5 . . . Were it in my power it should be ten times that sum . . . I am ever your affectionate grandfather, Job Heath.

As numbers grew so did the weekly offerings, and the paltry remuneration that had attended Brown's early preaching was replaced by an adequate stipend. At last in 1865 Archibald knew he could support Annie, and the two were married on 12 October. The following year, when Archibald was twenty-two, the new church was opened.

Shortly after the opening of the new building Brown preached a sermon on the text 'Young man, I say unto thee, Arise' (*Luke* 7:14). So certain was he of the power and blessing of God resting on that sermon that he announced that he would be in his vestry the following day and would be glad to see anyone brought under a sense of sin and in need of spiritual counsel. That Monday the young pastor waited hopefully in his vestry for the people to come and see him. Hour passed after hour and not one person arrived. And still he waited, until, in his own words:

I could bear it no longer, and I went out to the back of the chapel and, flinging myself down in the long rank grass, I writhed in anguish of soul. What a humiliation it was! Here had I announced I was sure there would be conversions, and not a soul came. I went home at nine o'clock worn out, feeling that I had been let down.

But not all was disappointment by far and the work in Bromley continued to grow steadily. Soon, however, Brown received a call to leave Bromley in order to take up the pastorate of the newly erected Stepney Green Tabernacle. A rapidly expanding work in the East End of London, this church had recently outgrown its former premises. Aided by the Metropolitan Tabernacle, a new and handsome building seating 800 people had been opened by Spurgeon at the end of 1864. And now, two years later, the church was searching for another pastor. Approaching Spurgeon for advice, the deacons were startled when he recommended a twenty-two-year old man for the onerous task – Archibald Brown. And to back up his recommendation,

[51]

Spurgeon assured the surprised deacons that he himself would be prepared to walk four miles to hear that young preacher – an accolade indeed, coming from a preacher such as Spurgeon.

Invited to preach at Spurgeon's midweek meeting one Thursday, Archibald Brown did not know that the deacons from Stepney Green were seated in the congregation listening attentively to his address. Although initially disconcerted by his boyish appearance, the deacons soon forgot Brown's youth as they heard him preach. Taking back a warm recommendation to the church, they invited him to preach at Stepney Green on two consecutive Sundays. Any hesitation soon evaporated, and Archibald Brown was invited to the pastorate in November 1866, to begin his ministry on the first Sunday of 1867.

Throughout January there were marked evidences of the presence of God accompanying the preaching of the new pastor. Each Sunday that month someone professed conversion. But 10 February was a never-to-be-forgotten date in the annals of Stepney Green. Aiming to influence men in particular on that occasion, Brown requested that the galleries be reserved for men only. A strange conviction persuaded him that he must repeat the sermon which he had preached earlier in Bromley, 'Young man, I say unto thee, Arise,' even though the results had been so disappointing before. As Brown concluded that sermon he recounted to his congregation, many of whom were indeed 'young men' how God had laid hold of him – a headstrong and feckless youth – and saved him. Over one hundred people were converted that night, ninety of whom Brown himself had the joy of baptising. How must the sound of trumpets echoed through the courts of heaven as the angels of God rejoiced over so signal a work of grace! For Brown himself, the gladness was tempered by a new understanding of God's ways. Now he knew why he had experienced such a degree of humiliation in Bromley. If ever he were tempted to glory in his own abilities, the salutary recollection of writhing in distress in the long grass behind the church in Bromley was enough to correct his thinking and ensure that he ascribed all the glory to God.

The start of this exceptional work of the Spirit of God among the people of East London, co-incided with days of revival in many other parts of the country. In seven years numbers had climbed from 294 when Brown had started in 1867 to well over 1000. Baptisms took place every week, sometimes sixty in one month. The only month in his thirty-year ministry when no baptisms were recorded was during a winter when all the water pipes were frozen!

Closely related to this steady and significant work of God was the time and priority given to prayer in the life of the church at Stepney Green. A prayer meeting was held after most Sunday evening services, and also one on each Monday evening. These meetings were both started and ended punctually, and Brown would not permit excessively long prayers – usually shorter but never longer than ten minutes – apart from exceptional circumstances. The prayer meetings that became the most memorable in the life of the church, however, were the great Saturday evening gatherings. When Archibald Brown first proposed holding these meetings, his deacons objected because this was the day that East End people did their evening shopping. But they came in their hundreds, many bringing their shopping with them so that a special room was allocated for shopping bags while the meeting was in progress. Chairs and benches had to be brought in to supplement the seating and still the people crowded in until there was scarcely any standing room. At last the fire hazard it presented caused the London County Council to step in and prohibit such overcrowding.

After four years at Stepney Green it became evident that the building was again too small for the burgeoning congregation. Designed to seat eight hundred, it was packed to the doors each Sunday, often thirteen hundred or more seeking admission. Even Annie failed to gain entrance on one occasion. Over six hundred had joined the membership, five hundred of these being new believers, converted and baptised under Archibald Brown's ministry. But where would the church find the finance for a building seating between two and three thousand? The cost price without any added profit was estimated at between £12,000-£13,000 – and the people of East London struggled constantly against poverty. Archibald's father, a bemused spectator of the results of his son's ministry, once again fretted. 'What do you think my son is going to do?' he exclaimed to another deacon of the Metropolitan Tabernacle – 'build a Tabernacle to hold three thousand people!'

'Then, Brown, if he says he will do it, he will, and the best thing we can do is to pray for him,' replied his wise fellow deacon.

'But where will the money come from?' persisted Archibald's father.

'Why, I expect he will come down on you first,' responded the other with undisguised glee.

And so it proved. On Archibald's first morning begging for contributions for his new project he started with a visit to a generous business friend. Announcing the purpose for his call, Brown could not fail to notice the look of dismay that crossed his friend's face.

'You've come at a very unfortunate time,' he admitted, 'I am afraid I can only give you a trifle. But if you will accept £500 [equivalent to at least £25,000 in present day values], you are very welcome to it.

Overjoyed at such a promising start, Brown called on another business friend who gave him £250. Arriving next at his father's home, he announced jubilantly, 'How much do you think I have received in the last forty minutes?'

'Oh, well, £20,' replied his father.

'No, £750,' replied his son, 'and as it is your birthday, I thought you might like to add £100 on the top, and then I shall go home satisfied with my morning's work!'

Spurgeon himself contributed £100 from his private funds, and by the end of the first month over £2,000 had been received. As the building fund increased, Brown's father caught the vision and eventually became one of his son's most generous supporters, personally contributing over £1,200 towards the projected East London Tabernacle.

Next, letters of appeal, 50,000 of them, were dispatched all over the world. In addition to describing the need, each letter also contained a printed sermon by the young preacher. Land was purchased on Burdett Road, which joined Mile End Road, a strategic position for reaching the teeming peoples crammed into London's East End. In April 1871 Archibald's father laid the foundation stone and in February 1872 Spurgeon preached the opening sermon in the vast new building – a structure that could seat 2,545 comfortably, but had extensions to allow a customary 3,200 to attend the services.

Outwardly Archibald Brown's life might appear a success story. But behind the scenes a dark shadow rested on Archibald and Annie's home life. Six children were born to the couple in quick succession: two sons and four daughters. But after only five years of married life, Annie was taken ill. Whether she was suffering from cancer we cannot now say, but for three years she suffered periods of intense pain, intermittent at first, but becoming prolonged and yet more acute as the months passed.

'If ever one went a rough road to glory; if ever one passed through a burning fiery furnace into heaven, she did,' said her husband. 'She knew what tears and groans and piteous cries meant.' So unbearable was her anguish that Archibald, a helpless spectator, could only pray, 'Lord, though it will make an unutterable blank, and though it means the breaking up of the happiest home that mortal man ever had, yet I could thank thee if thou wouldst take her into thine arms, and ease her of her frightful agonies.'

In May 1874, after only eight and a half years of marriage, Annie died. Just before she was taken she said to Archibald, who watched beside her, 'A few years at most and you and I will see each other again. To me it will seem only a minute or two, but I am dreadfully afraid it will seem a long time to you. Now I can sing a verse I never could sing before:

> *I have no cares, O blessed Lord,*
> *For all my cares are thine.'*

Gentle and unassuming by nature, Annie had been loved by the people whom she and her husband served unstintingly. At her funeral, traffic was at a standstill in all the main thoroughfares converging on Bow Cemetery for six hours, as the crowds gathered to pay their last respects to this tender-hearted and consistent Christian woman.

Annie's death left Archibald, only twenty-nine years of age, desolate. His own loneliness and needs were multiplied by the burden he carried of caring for his six motherless children all under the age of eight – and this in addition to the incessant demands of the ministry of the East London Tabernacle. The following year Archibald remarried. Sarah Hargreaves had been a close friend of Annie's and already knew the home and family. But this happiness too was short-lived, for within a year Sarah also died, together with the infant she had just borne to Archibald. This second bereavement following so closely upon the first appeared to prostrate him to an even greater degree. Unable to preach for some weeks, it seemed as if his nervous system had sustained a shattering blow. Spurgeon wrote in his monthly magazine, *The Sword and the Trowel*:

Mr Archibald Brown of the East London Tabernacle had been heavily bereaved. His second wife has been taken away, just when she seemed essential to his little ones, and to the church. His anguish is most acute, and we invite all our brethren to pray that he may be sustained, and enabled to pursue that wonderful career of usefulness for which our Lord has raised him up.

These prayers were answered to a remarkable degree as two months later Archibald Brown took up his ministry again. The years that followed became some of the most fruitful of his life and by 1882 the church membership had doubled from over 1000 to nearly 2,100.

Disciplined in the school of sorrows, the pastor of East London Tabernacle was able to reach out to the hearts of suffering people all around in a new way. The destitution and need he discovered in many East End homes stirred up in him a determination to do all in his power to bring physical relief wherever he could in addition to his faithful preaching of the gospel. After one particularly hard winter Archibald Brown was called to the deathbed of a young widow. Haunted by fears that her six-year-old son, Willie, would be taken to the workhouse as soon as she died, the woman clung desperately to life. As Brown entered the poverty-stricken home, the young mother turned in her bed and in pitiful tones begged the pastor to ensure that Willie would be cared for after her death. Remembering his own motherless children, Brown had no alternative but to promise that he would undertake for Willie's future. Out of the needs of this child grew the formation of several small orphan homes in connection with the East London Tabernacle. Over the years many needy children were cared for and equipped with a suitable training to enable them to find employment after they left the homes.

Nor was the provision for destitute children the only social work initiated by members of the East London Tabernacle under the guidance of their pastor. Church members regularly undertook distribution of food and clothing to hundreds of households where poverty, often exacerbated by alcohol, had left families in a state of impoverishment. As the years passed, teams of missioners went out from the Tabernacle bringing relief wherever they could.

Not every case was genuine, as some of the missionaries discovered. One parted with his last few shillings to a poor woman whom he found sitting disconsolately beside the sheet-covered body of her husband. She told him that he had died only hours previously and she had been laying him out. Not many minutes after leaving the house the missioner discovered he had left his umbrella behind. When he returned to collect it he found the woman looking much more cheerful – as did her husband who had removed the sheet and was sitting beside the fire.

Many were the stories Archibald Brown could tell of the relief work undertaken amongst the poor of London's East End; but his supreme confidence lay in the preaching of the gospel, which alone could transform and motivate men and women. 'Much as we love the poor, we could not toil the hours we do had we no deeper inspiration than the alleviation of their earthly wretchedness,' he commented on one occasion.

Above all Archibald Brown was a preacher of outstanding excellence. His natural eloquence prompted W. Robertson Nicol, a critic of no mean stature, to place on record in *The British Weekly* that in his estimation Brown was the greatest unrecognised orator in England at that time. Combining a splendid speaking voice, clear articulation and a gift for homely illustration, Brown held his East London congregations captive as he applied the Word of God to their consciences. Like those of his mentor and friend, Spurgeon, many of Brown's sermons had evocative titles, and in the three volumes of published addresses one can catch something of the impact they must have had on his first hearers. A sermon on heaven bore the title, *What is never said in heaven*. Taking for his text 'And the inhabitant shall not say, "I am sick": the people that dwell therein shall be forgiven their iniquity' (*Isa*. 33:24), he described the three types of sickness which would never distress the redeemed in glory. First, he spoke of bodily sickness and pain; then of heart sickness arising from disappointments, sorrows and unfulfilled longings; and lastly of soul sickness, those spiritual distresses brought about by guilt, unbelief, backslidings and the power of temptation. 'You thus see', he concluded, 'that all three kinds of sicknesses are absent from the New Jerusalem. "The inhabitant shall not say, 'I am sick.'" There will be no pain, no death, no bereavement, no heartache, no mental burden, no indwelling sin: all these belong to the past, the earth that is left behind.' Closing this sermon with an unexpected twist, he urged his people, in view of the joys in store for them, to do all in their power to relieve the sorrows and suffering evident on every hand in the dark areas of the capital so close to the church.

In a day when fearless gospel preaching was at a premium, Brown still dared to flout prevailing opinion by denouncing the evils of the human heart and extolling the merits of Christ's death as a substitute for the sins of his people. Speaking of him many years later, H. Tydeman Chilvers, a future minister of Spurgeon's Metropolitan Tabernacle, was to say:

What shall we say of his expository preaching, his exaltation of Christ, his holy greed for souls, his marked fidelity to the gospel, and his jealousy for the doctrines of grace? He was a love, blood and power preacher; one of God's valiant men and a mighty winner of souls.

And Captain Arthur Blackwood, under whose preaching Brown had been converted, could add:

Despising all sentimentalism and detesting anything like sensationalism, Archibald Brown has ever relied upon the old-fashioned gospel . . . and the Holy Spirit has honoured that simple reliance by using the message through his lips as the means of changing the hearts of thousands. Taking his stand on the doctrines of grace he has steadily held on his way, regardless of the philosophies and quackeries of those who would preach some other gospel as the remedy for the sins and sorrow and needs of men.

Brown's staunch adherence to the doctrines of grace brought him constant criticism and not a little cynical comment from the press. But even his severest critics could not deny that preaching these Calvinistic doctrines brought the blessing of God upon his ministry in East London, confounding the pundits. One newspaper wrote in 1891:

It is a great and good work, and the strangeness of it is that it is all associated with the narrowest theology, with a Calvinistic creed. As a preacher Mr Brown has few equals . . . Heaven and hell are awful realities to him . . . Apart from his noble social work he is the East End apostle of the most dismal gospel . . . That he should set up distress funds, homes for the poor, orphanages, convalescent homes is the beautiful contradiction [between] a good life and a sour creed. But so it is. Preaching an obsolete creed, ignoring the researches of science, regardless of biblical criticism, and expounding the Bible by the fading light of a dying theology, yet Mr A. G. Brown is in a sense a man of the times. He cares for the poor and exhausts the love of a large heart in trying to do good among the tens of thousands who crowd the narrow streets and dark alleys and courts down by way of Stepney, Mile End and Bow.

[60]

Not only did the press find fault with his preaching, but also some of his congregation. One man, so angered because his wife had professed conversion, decided to shoot the preacher. Mingling among the crowds the following Sunday, he found a strategic spot in the gallery to one side of the pulpit. There he waited with his loaded revolver. The best moment to strike would be in the prayer before the sermon when all the worshippers would have heads bowed and none would see him take his aim. So he had to wait through the reading of the Scripture, which following Spurgeon's custom, Brown would intersperse with telling comments. That night the reading was Isaiah 53. As the preacher commented on the Man of Sorrows, bruised and disfigured for the transgressions of his people, the would-be assassin found himself unable to shoot. Instead he went to the vestry after the service and, telling the preacher of his dark design, handed over his weapon.

Two years after the death of his second wife Archibald Brown once again knew the joy of marriage and the comforting presence of another to share his home and look after his six children, the eldest of whom was only twelve. Edith Barrett proved an excellent wife for the pastor of East London Tabernacle, supporting and caring for him for more than thirty years.

The 1880s were to prove difficult days for men prepared to stand against the tide of unbelief sweeping the Christian church. Many good men failed to see the issues at stake, while others were too weak to risk unpopularity by rising in defence of the revealed truths of Scripture. Still others capitulated to the prevailing opinions, drifting further and further into unbelief. When Spurgeon made his heroic and lonely stand against the encroaching error, which he discovered among churches and ministers belonging to the Baptist Union – that contention known as the Downgrade Controversy – few stood with him. But of the support of one man he had no doubts. Archibald Brown shared the same convictions and was prepared to stand by them, regardless of personal cost. Both Brown and his church withdrew from the London Baptist Association as well as the Baptist Union during 1888 – a course of action which brought upon him considerable criticism and, yet harder to bear, misunderstanding and expressions of sorrow from fellow pastors and other Christians who could see no necessity for the separation.

For Spurgeon, already an ill man, the controversy with all its recriminations undoubtedly hastened the course of his disease, bringing his life to a close at only fifty-seven years of age. Writing to Brown from Mentone on 2 January 1892, where he was convalescing after serious illness, Spurgeon expressed his gratitude to his friend for his unreserved support:

Beloved Brother, Receive the assurance of my heart-love, although you have no need of such an assurance from me. You have long been most dear to me; but in your standing shoulder to shoulder with me in protest against deadly error we have become more than ever one. The Lord sustain, comfort, perfect you! Debtors to free and sovereign grace, we will together sing to our redeeming Lord, world without end. Yours most heartily, C.H.SPURGEON

Little more than three weeks after writing those words, Spurgeon, set free from pain and the calumny of men, had already begun to sing that new song.

Like countless other men and women converted, challenged and encouraged through Spurgeon's remarkable ministry, Archibald Brown mourned deeply the loss of his friend. But to him fell the task, probably at once both the highest privilege and greatest responsibility of his life, to read the Scriptures at the funeral service, and yet more memorably, to deliver an oration at the graveside. Thousands packed Norwood Cemetery and heard his unforgettable words spoken with deep pathos and many pauses as he stood by the open grave of one who had been more than a friend to him:

Beloved President, Faithful Pastor, Prince of Preachers, Brother Beloved, Dear Spurgeon – we bid thee not 'Farewell' but only for a little while 'Good-night'. Thou shalt rise soon at the first dawn of the Resurrection-day of the redeemed. Yet is not the good night ours to bid but thine; it is we who linger in the darkness; thou art in God's holy light. Our night shall soon be past and with it all our weeping. Then, with thine, our songs shall greet the morning of a day that knows no cloud nor close; for there shall be no night there.

Hard worker in the field! Thy toil is ended, Straight has been the furrow thou hast ploughed. No looking back has marred thy course. Harvests have followed thy patient sowing, and heaven is already rich with thine ingathered sheaves, and shall be still enriched with years yet lying in eternity.

Champion of God! thy battle, long and nobly fought is over; the sword that clave to thy hand has dropped at last; a palm branch takes its place. No longer does the helmet press thy brow, oft weary with its surging thoughts of battle; a victor's wreath from the great Commander's hand has already proved thy full reward.

Here for a little while shall rest thy precious dust. Then shall thy Well-Beloved come; and at his voice thou shalt spring from thy couch of earth, fashioned like unto his body in glory. Then spirit, soul and body shall magnify thy Lord's redemption. Until then, Beloved, sleep. We praise God for thee, and by the blood of the everlasting covenant, hope and expect to praise God with thee. Amen.

Following the death of Spurgeon, Archibald Brown continued at East London Tabernacle for a further five years. But by the end of 1896, having completed thirty years as their pastor, during which time he had personally baptised over 5000 people on profession of faith, he concluded that his ministry there must now finish. At the age of fifty-two he could well have felt exhausted by the constant demands of so large a congregation. Following the conclusion of his pastorate, Archibald Brown and his wife spent the next few months together in America.

On his return, the simultaneous invitations of two churches to their pulpits, confronted him with a difficult choice. Wishing to remain in London, rather than to move to Folkestone on the coast, he accepted the call from Chatsworth Road Baptist Church in West Norwood. There Archibald Brown conducted a fruitful and satisfying ten-year ministry, seeing a previously ailing church blessed and reinvigorated as more than 1200 people were received into membership.

Now sixty-three years of age, Archibald Brown found much spiritual satisfaction in his family life. Following his marriage with Edith four more children were added to the family. A number of the older girls responded to the call of the foreign mission fields, exchanging the security of home life for a hazardous and stressful existence in far distant places. Best known of Archibald Brown's family was Douglas Brown, Annie's eldest son. Following his father into the Christian ministry, he was instrumental in establishing Balham Baptist Church through his preaching, and was soon privileged to play a key role in the significant revival in Lowestoft in 1921 – one of the last, though largely forgotten, revivals of the twentieth-century in Britain.

At such a time Archibald Brown might well have felt the attraction of a less onerous situation and opted for a quieter life. But at that very point came a yet more challenging call – an invitation to the Metropolitan Tabernacle itself, to become co-pastor with Thomas Spurgeon, who had been pastor since the year after his father's death. Failing now in health himself, Thomas felt the need of an assistant, and even though the East London Tabernacle, torn by internal bickering since Brown had left in 1897, also pressed him to return to them, he agreed to accept the call to the Metropolitan Tabernacle. The debt of love he owed to Spurgeon was clearly a determining consider-ation. And so in 1907 he began his ministry at the Tabernacle – for one year as co-pastor and then, when Thomas Spurgeon's deteriorating health forced him to resign though still only fifty-two years of age, Archibald Brown became the sole pastor.

For three and a half years Brown remained the pastor of the Tabernacle. The favour of God continued to rest on his preaching even though the tide of blessing was ebbing swiftly among English churches. During that period, over four hundred men and women professed faith and were received into membership.

But at the age of sixty-six, even this veteran in God's service knew he could go on no longer. His sorrowful people begged him to reconsider his decision to terminate his ministry there but he knew it was not to be. Replying to their persistent requests he wrote to the members:

With all my heart I thank you for your love in Christ Jesus. It is more precious than words can tell! With you I rejoice in all that the Lord has done, and if he has been pleased to make me a channel of blessing to any, to him be all the praise. I would gladly do anything you ask that is in my power, but your request to reconsider my decision is impossible . . . It is not the result of emotion but of conviction. It has been arrived at through no little heart agony, and the arguments of advancing age and ill health retain all their force.

And so came to an end a long and significant ministry of a preacher whose life and contribution would have marked him out as one of the best-known and remembered evangelical ministers of the nineteenth century in Britain, had he not been eclipsed by one of yet greater ability – C. H. Spurgeon himself.

Twelve years of life remained for Brown, years when he accepted an itinerant ministry as long as he had the strength, with notable periods in Dublin and in Sandown on the Isle of Wight; years too of travel, for he visited South Africa, Tasmania and New Zealand; and years of suffering as his health declined and he experienced the pain of yet another bereavement in the loss of his wife, Edith.

At last in April 1922, having been a glad witness of the revival in Lowestoft in which his son Douglas played so significant a part, God called his faithful servant home at the age of seventy-eight. Words that Archibald Brown himself had used to describe Spurgeon as he stood at his open graveside, could equally be applied to this earnest and greatly used preacher:

Hard worker in the field! Thy toil is ended, Straight has been the furrow thou hast ploughed. No looking back has marred thy course. Harvests have followed thy patient sowing, and heaven is already rich with thine ingathered sheaves, and shall be still enriched with years yet lying in eternity.

Buried in Easton-on-Hill, Northamptonshire, Archibald Brown's own epitaph fittingly reads: *A servant of Jesus Christ; and God's messenger to multitudes of people.*

JOHN NELSON
Yorkshire Evangelist

4

A child of nine sat on the floor with other members of his family listening to his father read from the Bible.

'And I saw a great white throne and him that sat thereon, from whose face the heavens and earth fled away . . . and the books were opened and another book was opened which is the book of life . . .'

The boy started to tremble involuntarily. Years later he recalled that it seemed as if a sharp arrow had pierced through him. He began to cry quietly, but as his father read on, his agitation became more acute. He plugged his fingers into his ears, but still he could hear his father's voice: 'and the dead were judged out of those things that were written in the books, according to their works . . .'

Young John Nelson could bear no more. Falling face forward on the floor, he began to sob uncontrollably. Before his vivid imagination flashed the sight of men and women approaching that awesome throne, each comparing his life's record against God's entry in the book; and then moving away to an eternal destiny. Whether John's father ever understood the cause of his child's distress that day, we do not know. Certainly the boy had no one to direct him from the demands of a righteous Judge to a merciful Saviour.

Born in 1707 in Birstall, then only a village near Leeds in West Yorkshire, John Nelson grew to adulthood in the days immediately prior to the Evangelical Revival of the eighteenth century. Prior to this only pockets of gospel light had shone here and there in that extensive county, but for the most part, the people had lived and died without any saving knowledge of God. But during the early years of that century some remarkable children were born: Charles Wesley and the Countess of Huntingdon in that same year as Nelson; John Wesley four years earlier, William Grimshaw the year after, and George Whitefield in 1714. All these were being prepared by God for that new day of his grace soon to dawn, but for the present there was no one to instruct young John Nelson in the truth.

Clearly John Nelson's father was a God-fearer but probably unable to help his son. Nor could John shrug off the fears and sense of accountability created in his conscience that day. Throughout his teenage years he found 'a hell in my mind' whenever he was conscious of having done wrong. But his secret grief and resolutions to improve quickly evaporated as soon as he was back in the company of his peers when he would plunge once more into his course of evil.

Strange dreams also troubled the young man. One dream in particular when he was sixteen perplexed him and left an unforgettable impression on him. He was standing with the prophet Jeremiah outside the walls of Jerusalem listening to God's fearless messenger reproving the wicked city. He saw the hapless man thrown on a rubbish heap where butchers disposed of the offal from their meat there to be trampled underfoot. Jeremiah's courage filled the dreamer with such admiration that he found himself crying out, 'O God, make me like Jeremiah!' – a dream which he would have good cause to recollect in future years.

At the age of nineteen John Nelson stood at a critical juncture of his life. Forgetting his earlier religious impressions, he had been imitating the godless and dissolute lifestyle of his compatriots. Either he could continue in that course – a way of life dictated by his own sinful nature, leading to a life of dissipation, or he could seek God earnestly for the gift of an upright girl to marry – one with whom he could live in a manner pleasing to God. He chose the latter. At this time Nelson was following his father's trade and had become a stonemason, learning the skill of hewing and shaping stones for churches and other buildings. And as the young man worked he prayed, not once but many times over, that God would allow him to meet honourable girl. Toiling one day on a new church building, John Nelson spotted a young woman whom he had never seen before. Without even enquiring her name or background, he resolved at once that this girl was the answer to his prayers and that he would marry her. And he did.

If he imagined that marriage to Martha would quieten his troubled conscience, John Nelson soon discovered his mistake. His old dissatisfaction and sense of failure followed him into his married life, robbing him of any peace. Each attempt at reformation – failing as it inevitably did – added to his frustration until at last Nelson decided that a change of environment might provide an answer. He would leave Martha in Yorkshire and seek work in London. For six months he did this, but peace of conscience still eluded the troubled man. Returning home, he was soon as unsettled as ever and suggested to Martha that this time they would both go to live in London. And always in the back of his mind he hoped that some change of circumstance might at last bring the answers to the insistent questions concerning his eternal destiny.

Here he and Martha lived for some years, and two children were born. When Martha's health began to deteriorate, however, they agreed together that she should return to Yorkshire with the children and he would follow when his current employment ended. Back in Yorkshire once more,

John Nelson still could not settle. Unable to sleep at night, he was pursued by the same sense of futility and failure. 'I was yet as a man in a barren wilderness, that could find no way out,' he wrote as he later described these days. At last he decided he must return to London, this time on his own. Without his family he could travel more easily from place to place, from church to church seeking answers to his unrest of conscience. This he did, but all his efforts seemed futile. Some sermons even increased his despair as he was urged to look for salvation on the basis of the quality of his life. Remembering the horror of 'the great white throne' from his childhood days, he began to wish he had never been born, or that he had been created as a sheep or cow with no accountability before God for its ways.

Finding no help from the Established churches, he tried the Dissenters, the Quakers and even the Catholics. But God's day for this troubled young man was approaching. In 1739 the twenty-five-year-old George Whitefield had begun preaching to vast crowds on Kennington Common and Moorfields. Joining the throng, Nelson highly appreciated the preaching he heard, even being ready to raise his fists in the preacher's defence if necessary: but even so he did not understand his message.

Then one day Nelson heard a preacher at Moorfields whom he had never seen before. The story is best told in his own words:

I was like a wandering bird cast out of its nest till Mr John Wesley came to preach his first sermon at Moorfields. O! that was a blessed morning to my soul! As soon as he got upon the stand, he stroked back his hair and turned his face towards where I stood, and I thought fixed his eyes upon me. His countenance struck such an awful dread upon me, before I heard him speak, that it made my heart beat like the pendulum of a clock; and when he did speak, I thought his whole discourse was aimed at me. When he had done, I said, 'This man can tell the secrets of my heart: [but] he hath not left me there; for he hath showed the remedy, even the blood of Jesus.

Hesitantly John Nelson tried to follow the path to God pointed out by this new preacher. He prayed diligently, read the Scriptures and avoided the company of his godless friends. But Satan would not easily release this man from his grip. Nelson records:

But my old companions missed me, and came to see what was the matter. When they found me reading the Bible they cursed and swore, and dragged me away to an alehouse, where I sat down and began to reason with them. But O! how dangerous it is to encounter Satan on his own ground! For as I talked I began to drink a little, and the liquor getting to my head I quarrelled and fought, and as I was going to my quarters a lewd woman met me and I had no power to resist her, and was again taken captive by the devil.

Back on his old course, Nelson now experienced an added measure of despair gripping him. But God intended to rescue this man, and he felt himself continually drawn back to hear the Wesley brothers preach time after time.

The crisis came some weeks later. Having failed once again, Nelson now knew of no expedient that could save him from eternal destruction – nothing apart from the undeserved mercy of God:

I then went into my chamber and shut the door and fell down on my knees crying, 'Lord, save me or I perish!' When I had prayed until I could pray no more, I got up and walked to and fro, being resolved I would neither eat nor drink until I had found the kingdom of God. I went to prayer again but found not relief, got up and walked again: then tears began to flow from my eyes like great drops of rain, and I fell on my knees a third time; but now I was dumb and could not put up one petition, if it would have saved my soul. I kneeled before the

Lord some time and saw myself a criminal before the Judge: then I said, 'Lord, Thy will be done; damn or save.' That moment Jesus Christ was evidently set before the eyes of my mind as crucified for my sins . . . and in that instant my heart was set at liberty from guilt and tormenting fear, and filled with a calm and serene peace.

Made new by the grace of God, John Nelson lost no time in testifying to his former friends and companions of the transforming power of God, urging them too to repent of sin while mercy could be found. He was not popular. His landlady was prepared to put him onto the street, his employers wished to terminate his contract because he refused to work on Sunday, and the enemy of his soul tormented him with terrifying dreams. But by God's help Nelson steadfastly maintained his stand. Now he wanted nothing more than to return to Martha and share the blessings he had known. After he had completed his tasks in London, he wrote to Yorkshire telling her of all that had taken place and informing her of his intentions.

Martha Nelson welcomed her husband home but was little prepared for the change in him. Filled with a new joy, and with all the old restlessness of spirit gone, he now longed to lead his family and neighbours into the same truths that had transformed his life. Without hesitation he reproved the glaring sins and prevailing godlessness he discovered all around him. Martha was acutely embarrassed and distressed. With her husband acting in this way she dared not even leave the house for fear of the neighbours' tongues. She began to wish he had stayed in London, and at last issued an ultimatum that unless he could stop offending everyone she would not be able to live with him any longer.

But Nelson's earnest exhortations were being accompanied by an unusual power. Within three weeks of his arrival seventeen of his family and neighbours had been converted. From far and near the curious, the anxious and the belligerent crowded into Martha's home to debate with the stonemason, for the concept of an assurance of forgiveness for sin was a novel and scarcely-known doctrine at that time. Only Martha remained untouched. Accusing John of not loving her any longer, she cried, 'My happiness with thee is over; for according to thy words, I am a child of the devil and thou a child of God.' Despite John's protestations of his increased affection for Martha, she only wept and said, 'I cannot live with thee.'

Nevertheless, John gave himself to prayer and fasting for his wife's conversion, assuring her, 'I believe God will hear my prayer and convert thy soul, and make thee a blessed companion for me in the way to heaven.' And God did hear his prayer; for not long afterwards during a time of serious illness, Martha was brought to realise that unless Christ intervened and saved her soul she would perish for ever in the abyss of God's righteous judgments against sin. Healed as it were in a moment, both physically and spiritually, Martha Nelson supported her husband unwaveringly from that day onwards in spite of the heavy sufferings it brought upon her and her family.

John Nelson's routine was an exacting one. As soon as he had finished his daily work quarrying and chiselling stones, and without waiting for a meal, he would hurry off to some appointed place where a group of people had gathered to hear his new teaching. Still clad in his working clothes – for he possessed little else – and with his chisel slung at his waist, he would exhort his hearers to repentance and faith. In this way, without design or intent, Nelson became one of the earliest lay preachers of the Evangelical Revival.

John Nelson was not the only man whom God had raised up to bring the light of the gospel to Yorkshire at this time. Benjamin Ingham, a member of the Holy Club in Oxford

– that group of men who by austerity, diligence and good works strove to gain acceptance with God, had accompanied John and Charles Wesley to the New World in 1735. Enlightened and truly converted through the influence of some Moravians he had met on the journey, Ingham had returned in 1737 to his home in Ossett, not far from Birstall. From there he travelled throughout the towns and villages of the west Yorkshire, preaching and forming his converts into societies for mutual encouragement and fellowship.

When Ingham heard of the stonemason who had turned to preaching in his spare moments, he might well have been offended, for Nelson was neither ordained nor trained. But after asking to speak to the earnest young man, Ingham was large-hearted enough to recognise all that God was accomplishing through him and to welcome him to preach among his societies whenever he wished. Sadly the relationship was short-lived, for not long after, Ingham fell under the influence of erroneous thinking newly introduced amongst the Moravians. Teaching that enquirers and even converts who lacked assurance should cease attending the means of grace and just be still until God gave them faith, these ideas cut at the heart of Nelson's evangelistic efforts. Ingham's early debt of gratitude to the Moravians made him susceptible to such an influence, and having accepted it at least temporarily himself, he withdrew his fellowship from Nelson.

Nothing daunted, Nelson continued to labour all day and preach to the crowds who thronged to hear him each evening. But he often felt alone and thought wistfully of John and Charles Wesley preaching in London. He longed to see them again. One night early in 1742 he dreamt that these two men were actually sitting on either side of his own fireplace, and that John Wesley said he was going north but would visit Birstall again on his return. Recounting his dream to a friend the following day, Nelson passed the comment that such an event was no more likely than a visit from the king. But so it happened. Four months later, after Nelson had written a letter to John Wesley introducing himself and telling him of all that God had been doing in Yorkshire, Wesley decided to visit the earnest stonemason and on his first visit to Newcastle broke his journey at Birstall. Sitting in exactly the same posture as Nelson had seen in his dream, Wesley assured the Yorkshireman that he would pay him a longer visit on his return from Newcastle. This marked the beginning of a close and lifelong co-operation between the faithful stonemason-preacher and the early Methodist movement.

But the days were rough, and the people, often living in deprived and degrading circumstances, could easily be aroused to violate and abuse the brave preacher. With passion enflamed by cheap gin, troublemakers would mingle among the crowds gathered to hear Nelson. In Nottingham a succession of homemade fireworks were hurled at Nelson as he preached from the Market Cross. Time after time God's protecting care delivered the preacher from injury as each burning missile seemed deflected by an unseen hand. At last the arch-perpetrator of this assault, an army sergeant, approached Nelson in tears saying, 'In the presence of God and all this people, I beg your pardon, for I came on purpose to mob you . . . but . . . am convinced of the deplorable state my soul is in, and I believe you are a servant of the living God.' Embracing the preacher, he turned back into the crowd with tears streaming down his face.

Martha Nelson, who courageously supported her husband, shared the vicious and mindless persecution. Returning on one occasion from nearby Wakefield together with a few other women, she became aware that she was being followed by a threatening mob. With a pregnancy far advanced, she had every reason to be apprehensive, but at last turned to address the rabble who were clearly intent on causing trouble. The men, ashamed of themselves, slunk away, but a group of women continued to follow. As Martha and her friends approached a gate, a cry was heard, 'You are Nelson's wife, and here you shall die.' Then they kicked and beat Martha with such malice that on reaching home she gave birth to a dead infant. She never fully recovered from the injuries she sustained that day. When John returned he was shocked and distressed by all that Martha had endured, but was able to write, 'This treatment she had reason to remember to her life's end; but God more than made it up to her by filling her with peace and love.'

In 1744 yet more troubles were in store for John and Martha Nelson. Behind the most inveterate enemies of the early Methodist preachers there could often be found the local clergy into whose parishes these messengers of the gospel had dared to venture. The vicar of Birstall was no exception. Angered by the enthusiasm with which the people gathered to hear this upstart, as he regarded Nelson, preaching on his patch, he determined to put an end to such an infringement of his rights by arranging to have the stonemason arrested as a malingerer and press-ganged into the army. He had little difficulty, for in February of that year there had been an abortive attempt on the part of the Young Pretender to land an invasion force. Suspicions and fears were therefore running high.

Under a strange apprehension that trouble was near, Nelson continued to work and preach as usual, but one day a verse of Scripture kept ringing in the back of his mind: 'I, even I, am he that comforteth you: who art thou that thou shouldest be afraid of a man that shall die . . . Fear not, I am with thee.' And so Nelson toiled on at his work and that night hurried to Adwalton where he was due to preach. But as the people were dispersing he felt a heavy hand on his shoulder. The deputy-constable, who also kept a tavern and therefore found his trade under threat by the changed lives of Nelson's converts, arrested the preacher and led him away. Normally men press-ganged for military duties were afforded an opportunity to vindicate their characters and explain why such an arrest was wrongful. No such option was allowed to this despised Methodist preacher. Calling briefly at his home the next day, Nelson was permitted to gather a few items of clothing before being marched off, first to Halifax and then on to Bradford. No refreshment was granted, nor was any clemency afforded, though £500 was offered for his bail.

That night a quick kangaroo court was assembled, and though Nelson defended himself stoutly against charges of debt and idleness, his defence fell on deaf ears, and he was thrown into a dungeon below a local abattoir. A stinking hovel, it was contaminated by stale blood that had seeped through the floor boards allowing Nelson space neither to sit nor to lie. Not a drink of water to alleviate his thirst was allowed for the suffering man. Yet even in this appalling situation, John Nelson was later able to say: 'My soul was so filled with the love of God that it was a paradise to me.' Perhaps he could almost catch the distant sound of the trumpeters of God as they celebrated the triumphs of faith over nature and circumstance; for such joy flooded his being that he cried out, 'O the glorious liberty of the children of God!' Kneeling down amid the filth, he praised God for allowing him to come to such a place for the truth's sake and found himself praying that those who had engineered these conditions for him might be as happy in their own beds as he was in his dungeon.

Although Martha was once again expecting a child and nearing her confinement, she rose that same night and walked the seven or more miles to Bradford, bringing with her a little food and drink. At four in the morning she arrived and, quickly enquiring for his whereabouts, made her way to the cellar prison. Through a hole in the door they began to speak. 'Jeremiah's lot is fallen on me,' confessed Nelson, recalling his dream and aspirations as a youth. Martha managed to pass the refreshments through the hole and encouraged him with the following remarkable words: 'Fear not, the cause is God's for which you are here, and he will plead it himself. Therefore, be not concerned for me and the children; he that feeds the young ravens will be merciful to us: he will give you strength for your day and after we have suffered awhile, he will perfect that which is lacking in our souls, and then bring us "where the wicked cease from troubling and the weary are at rest".' Supported by the knowledge of Martha's fortitude, Nelson responded stoutly, 'I cannot fear either man or devil, so long as I find the love of God as I do now'.

News of these events travelled swiftly from place to place for by now Nelson was a familiar figure in these Yorkshire towns. By five o'clock that morning he was hurried to Leeds, but the people, already crowding the streets to watch him pass shouted support or added their taunts. After a few days at Leeds the prisoner was marched to York, where again the streets were thronged with spectators. The crowds heaped abuse on Nelson, but upheld by God's special grace, he was able to pray, 'O, be merciful to this great city whose streets ring with curses, and turn upon them a pure language that they might be saved.' Here after a brief appearance at a military court, Nelson was assigned to the army, despite all protests that his conscience forbade him to take up weapons to harm his fellow men. Once again Martha was able to contact him in York, some twenty-five miles from her home, and add further encouragements to her husband, exhorting him to endure steadfastly to the end.

From York Nelson was stationed with the army in various northern towns, and always he bought up every opportunity to preach to the coarse military community and to many others who would otherwise never hear the gospel of God's grace. Travelling ever further north Nelson sturdily maintained his testimony, preaching wherever he had opportunity, while still submitting to the disciplines imposed upon him. Wherever the army was billetted, God raised up those who would sustain and encourage his servant, despite the opposition. At Durham he even managed a short meeting with John Wesley. 'Speak and spare not,' urged Wesley, 'for God hath work for you to do in every place where your lot is cast: and when you have fulfilled his good pleasure, he will break your bonds in sunder, and we shall rejoice together.' Further north still to Sunderland Nelson was taken, but there it was that God had ordained his release through the personal intervention of the Countess of Huntingdon with Lord Stair, the Earl of Sunderland. And on 28 July 1744, after ten weeks or more of captivity, the brave stonemason preacher was free to return to Yorkshire.

Welcomed home by many who had found spiritual life through his message, John Nelson flung himself fully into the labours of an itinerant preacher. Giving up his labours as a stonemason that he might give himself wholly to the task of preaching, he and Martha became dependent on the support of the small societies of believers brought into being through his preaching. Under the supervision of John Wesley, we catch glimpses of Nelson travelling the length and breadth of the country. But the life of an itinerant Methodist preacher was hard and fraught with dangers. A short letter from Charles Wesley to Nelson soon after his release from the army exhorted him in these words: 'My brother, you must watch, pray, labour and suffer.' These four words could summarize the next thirty years of Nelson's eventful life. Whether in Newcastle or Cornwall, Yorkshire or Lincolnshire, the first three were his all-consuming occupations and the last the consequence, as he preached ceaselessly wherever he could find opportunity.

On one occasion a mob near Leeds, enflamed by the local parson's son, determined to drown the fearless preacher. Grabbing him, they intended to fasten a halter round his neck, drag him to the river and throw him in. But as they attempted to fasten the halter their plot was foiled both by a sudden panic that swept over the chief perpetrator and by the appearance on the scene of the local constable.

Not long afterwards a hit man was hired to murder Nelson. In this he nearly succeeded. A colossal man, he leapt on the preacher. Nelson managed to escape the impact of his first and second attempts, but on the third was thrown to the ground. With his huge weight his assailant knelt on Nelson's stomach, crushing him until his victim appeared to be dead. 'Gentlemen, I have killed the preacher: he lies dead in the croft,' boasted the hit-man. But at this point even Nelson's enemies became fearful of the consequences of their misdeed, and discovering he was still alive, moved the injured man to a nearby house.

As the years passed and the effects of the revival became more widespread, such incidents decreased. In 1750 Nelson was back at his old employment of hewing stones, but not now for his own livelihood. This time he was building a small chapel in Birstall. Fully realising that a time might come when the converts from his preaching could be excluded from their own churches, he was anxious to provide a preaching house, as these chapels were called, where Methodists could worship unmolested. William Grimshaw from nearby Haworth, who had worked closely with Nelson since 1747, preached the first sermon in the uncompleted building in August 1750.

But while persecutions became less intense, Nelson and his family had other trials to face, more subtle and therefore more difficult to withstand. Preachers who gave up their means of supporting their families in order to preach the gospel often lived in extreme poverty. Although the early Methodists made some attempts to meet the needs of their preachers, such provision was often pitifully inadequate. Writing to Charles Wesley in 1758, Nelson describes his embarrassment:

This part I would have you keep to yourself . . . the stewards have sent me a letter that I must expect no more help from them; and we have but ten shillings a week in all, and that is to keep a servant out of [Martha's health had been broken by her sufferings] and wages to pay her which takes four shillings at least out of it. And we have coals and candles for the house, and soap to find, which will take two more, and all the goods in the house to keep in repair; and my meat when in the round, and in my absence another preacher for it; so that my family hath not one shilling a week to find them both meat and clothes, so that I am going to hew stone again. . . O sir, pray for me that I faint not at the last. This keeps my head above water to see that God continues to convert sinners by my word . . . so that I think he will either provide or take us to himself.

The sufferings and privation John Nelson had endured for the gospel's sake had indeed taken a heavy toll on his health. At sixty-two years of age he could scarcely walk without help and was obliged to lean on another man to support him whilst he was preaching. But the sight of their preacher, prematurely aged and infirm, filled his hearers with affection and gratitude as he continued to maintain his ministry for a further five years. No more was John Nelson the object of violent assault and abuse: rather he was loved by the people for all that God had accomplished through his faithful preaching over the years. Writing of him many years after his death Mary Fletcher, wife of John Fletcher the saintly vicar of Madeley, was to say, 'He was an extraordinary man for tenderness of conscience, watchfulness over his words, and especially for self-denial and rigid temperance. He made it a rule to rise out of his bed about twelve o'clock and sit up till two for prayer and converse with God: then he slept until four, at which time he always rose.'

In 1774 Nelson was stationed back in his own home area of Leeds. His friends noticed with satisfaction that despite physical weakness his preaching was warm and powerful and his personal conversation lively and sparkling. Nelson himself felt particularly well, commenting that he had not felt so fit for a long time.

But the end came suddenly. Appearing to be stricken with a violent stomach complaint when he returned from preaching one day, it became evident to his family and friends that this faithful pioneer preacher was being taken from them. Within two hours God had called his courageous servant away from all his labours and trials.

Two days later Leeds witnessed a funeral such as it had never seen before – itself an eloquent testimony to the effectiveness of John Nelson's labours. Thousands lined the route along which the coffin was slowly carried. Weeping and singing hymns composed by Charles Wesley, they followed their hero-preacher's coffin to the parish church at Birstall. And two months later his long-suffering wife Martha also finished her pilgrimage and followed him to that land of joy she had anticipated long ago as she stood outside his abattoir prison – a land 'where the wicked cease from troubling and the weary are at rest.'

Colonel James Gardiner

Christian Watt, her mother, Mary Noble, and her cousin Mary Watt

Archibald Brown

John Nelson

Dr Tom Barnardo

Samuel Pearce

The kitchen at Charles and Sally Wesley's house in Bristol

Their music room (photos courtesy of John Wesley's Chapel, Bristol)

DR. BARNARDO
The Children's Champion

5

'**A** bit of all sorts' was the way Tom Barnardo used to describe his nationality in terms of the blood that ran in his veins. Born in Dublin in 1845, Tom had an English mother whose family had long been resident in Ireland. His father, however, John Barnardo, who had settled in Dublin some years before Tom's birth and had become a prosperous business man, claimed Turkish, German, Spanish and Italian ancestry. Perhaps it was this mix that produced in Tom so quixotic, lively and unpredictable a temperament.

Tom's childhood days gave little promise of the man he would become and the purposes God had in store for his life. Underweight and frail at birth, his hold on life was tenuous during his early years. At the age of two his family all but lost him. Watching anxiously over their sick boy, his parents recognised with heavy hearts that the child's life was slipping away. At last the doctor in attendance pronounced him dead. A second doctor confirmed the sad news, and no option remained for the grieving parents but to call in an undertaker. With the coffin made and already waiting in the house, the undertaker began to prepare the child's body for burial. Suddenly he became conscious of a tiny flutter of movement, then another. Tom Barnardo was not dead. Gradually, very gradually, he was nursed back to health and grew to become a sturdy and resilient youngster. Snatched back from the very gates of death, this child was destined in God's plan to rescue many another young life from conditions which could only be called a living death.

Young Tom, the ninth in the family, was a difficult child. Described as 'hot tempered, self-willed and highly imperious', he had wiry hair, plain features and a voice remarkable only for its volume. Far different was Harry, Tom's younger brother, who with his fair hair, attractive features and beautiful singing voice charmed all who came to the home. Often called from his play to sing to the guests, Harry soon aroused Tom's animosity, particularly as his performances were usually rewarded with chocolates. On one occasion Harry was returning from the sitting room where he had just been singing to an admiring circle of visitors – and also finishing off the last of the chocolates that had been donated to him. Tom's fury knew no bounds. Delivering a well-aimed blow at his younger brother's face, he yelled, 'Take that for showing off in the drawing room!' And as Harry reeled from the impact, Tom delivered another with the words, 'And *that,* you pig, for eating all the chocolates yourself!'

Tom Barnardo's volatile and mischievous nature, made his school reports sorry reading. His endless chatter earned for his section of the class the designation of 'Prater's Row'. Recalling those days an older brother, Dr Frederick Barnardo wrote: 'He was full of fun, mischief, thoughtless and careless. Do not suppose he was born a saint and always a saint. He gave a good deal of trouble at home and had a very strong, determined self-will. At his first school he gave no end of trouble and at [his second] school was no better.' A fact his brother omitted to mention, however, was that at one of his schools Tom Barnardo had, as he was later to write, 'sat under the thraldom of one of the biggest and most brutal of bullies – the most cruel man, as well as the most mendacious, that I have ever met in all my life'. Children less resilient than Tom suffered severely at the hands of this schoolmaster. But the cruelty meted out to some of his peers which the boy witnessed gave rise in Tom Barnardo's mind to 'such intense loathing and disgust' of cruelty – an attitude extending to all forms of oppression of the weak and helpless – that he would carry with him as a motivating force throughout his life.

By the age of fourteen a more serious side of his nature began to emerge and reading became his predominant delight, though his school books still remained low in his list of priorities. Instead he chose philosophical and rationalistic writers and the concepts of Jacques Voltaire, Jean-Jacques Rousseau and Thomas Paine moulded his thinking. At fifteen years of age he declared himself an agnostic, firmly rejecting any religious impressions he had imbibed from his mother, who came from a Quaker family, or from the Church of Ireland, into which he had been baptised as an infant. His confirmation that same year was, therefore, a mere formality with no spiritual relevance for Tom. Organised Christianity became the butt of his unbelieving innuendoes, and even the Bible itself provided material for young Barnardo's cynical witticisms.

Small in build, bespectacled and with a reputation as a practical joker, Barnardo left school at the age of sixteen with few academic attainments. His father procured a position for him in clerical work in Dublin, and here his innate abilities began to show, even though an increasing love of reading made the discipline of office life irksome.

The early 1860s were momentous years for the gospel of Christ in Ireland. Repercussions from a powerful revival of religion that had begun in New York in 1858 had reached across the Atlantic and had affected Northern Ireland profoundly during 1859. And now the crowded streets and homes of Dublin were being touched by the transforming message of the grace of God in Christ. Vast numbers gathered in the Metropolitan Hall, formerly a circus arena, to listen to the preaching of men like Henry Grattan Guinness.

Tom Barnardo had little time for such things. Armed with the arguments of Voltaire and Rousseau, he had an answer for all the amazing events taking place around him. 'Emotional hysteria,' the arrogant seventeen-year-old called it, predicting that converts of the revival, some of them his former friends, would soon revert to their old habits. But beneath the surface young Barnardo was more troubled than he liked to admit, for even to his own mind his rationalistic explanations did not fully account for all he saw and heard around him. And then the conquering power of the gospel of Christ came too close for comfort. Two of Tom Barnardo's older brothers were converted.

Concerned for their younger brother, these two new converts urged Tom to accompany them to the meetings. But to no avail. Still they pleaded until at last he agreed to attend a smaller gathering in a private home – though his purpose was largely to disrupt the meeting with cheeky interjections. This he did, and describing his behaviour on that occasion many years later in a letter to the speaker at that meeting, he was to write, 'I behaved very badly. I was just as cheeky as a young fellow can be.' But instead of dealing with him as he knew he deserved, the leader had spoken kindly to the impudent young man. This disturbed Barnardo far more than angry words could have done. What if his brothers were right and he wrong? he pondered.

Despite his bravado this seed of doubt began to grow in Barnardo's mind and for the first time he questioned the presuppositions of his rationalistic reading material. No longer did he mock the religious convictions of his brothers and friends but instead could be found regularly attending the meetings himself. Not many weeks later one message pierced through Barnardo's soul like a knife. Now he knew for certain that not only was he wrong, but he had deeply offended against his God. No sleep could he find that night. And in the small hours of the morning a weary and burdened young man crept into the room where his older brothers were sleeping. Many were the tears shed as his brothers tried to help him, for he was in much distress of soul. But before dawn broke, as the three knelt in prayer together, the tears were replaced by light, joy and peace from God. Tom Barnardo now knew himself forgiven for his sins and reconciled to God through faith in the Saviour, crucified to pay the punishment that his sins well merited.

The change was immediate and obvious. Now the dust began to gather on Barnardo's former favourite books. Instead the Bible, previously the subject of many a joke, offered constant delight as he studied its pages. Joining a group of Plymouth Brethren, he found fellowship and encouragement in the company of like-minded Christians also quickened to zeal and service by the revival.

Under the guidance of his new friends he began to study the question of baptism and soon felt convinced that it was his duty to be immersed as a true believer. Entries in his diary during October 1862 – days that led up to this significant event in Barnardo's life – reveal his joyful spirit:

Oh Lord! I can never thank thee enough for all thy kindness and mercy to me, who am so unworthy to receive the very least of them. I have passed a delightful evening at home reading the Word of God. My heavenly Father has indeed been with me whilst reading the sacred volume, for my soul is as a giant refreshed with wine . . . Oh, I felt so happy, I cannot describe the joy which pervaded my heart at thus being able to testify Christ before all.

Nor could he keep the joy of his new-found peace with God to himself. With tireless zeal he flung himself into Christian service, enrolling as a teacher in a ragged school in one of Dublin's slums – an appalling contrast to the downtown areas of the city with their attractive new public buildings. For the first time he came face to face with the degrading poverty in which many families lived, particularly where whisky drinking in the home had drained its meagre resources. 'Had I a dog,' he declared, 'I would not kennel it where I found these immortal souls.'

Realising that social relief alone could not solve the problem of the 'fever dens and moral contagion' which so shocked him, Tom Barnardo and several of his brothers rented two rooms in an area where 'superstition, ignorance and whisky' had taken their heaviest toll. Here, despite local opposition, he made his first attempts at preaching and not without spiritual fruit.

But Tom Barnardo did not cast off all the characteristics of his quick-tempered nature in a moment. Formerly he had carried a cane wherever he went, now he dared do so no longer lest the objectionable behaviour of some of his pupils provoked him into using his stick.

For four years following his conversion Tom Barnardo continued at his secular employment, but although he gained promotion his heart was elsewhere. At last in February 1866 came a watershed in his life. Now nearly twenty-one, he had for some months attended a Bible class for young men which gathered regularly in the home of Henry Grattan Guinness, newly returned to his native Dublin from his preaching tours.

One evening Guinness announced that he had arranged for 'a great man' to address his class, none other than Dr James Hudson Taylor, back from China and seeking to rouse awareness among the Christian public to the wide open opportunities for the gospel in that vast and unknown land. Anticipation ran high as the young men waited for this distinguished missionary to appear. At last they heard he had arrived and looked up expectantly. There framed in the doorway was Grattan Guinness's ample and handsome form, but not a sign of the missionary. Had he failed to come after all? Then behind the erect form of their leader the waiting group caught sight of the slim youthful figure of the 'great' missionary. Astonished silence was the only welcome Hudson Taylor received. At last Barnardo broke the tension by declaring in an audible whisper, 'There's hope for me yet.'

But all was to change as Hudson Taylor addressed the group. Enthralled, they listened to his description of the limitless openings for Christian work in that far off land; they learnt of its social problems and the lack of men and women willing to sacrifice home and comfort for the gospel's sake. Engrossed by all he heard, Barnardo was so deeply stirred that before the evening was over he and three other young men had volunteered for missionary service in China. Though attracted by Barnardo's enthusiasm and mercurial personality, Hudson Taylor wisely wanted to allow the lapse of time to prove his zeal. So ten weeks later, at Taylor's suggestion, the young man found himself travelling to London to begin a period of training for missionary service.

Coborn Street, in the East End of London, was the destination to which the missionary candidate was appointed Here he was to spend time in the study of the Scriptures and to receive instruction in missionary principles. Despite a full schedule, Barnardo immediately sought opportunities to influence those he discovered all around him in the East End, often living in squallid and poverty-stricken conditions. Before many weeks had passed he had volunteered to help in nearby Ernest Street School, where deprived children were given a basic education similar to that of the 'ragged' schools of Dublin.

Monitoring the progress of his trainee missionary, Hudson Taylor was quick to note his unusual gifts and felt he would be even better equipped for service in China if he had some specific medical training. So it was that in October 1866, after only a few months in London,

Barnardo enrolled as a medical student at the London Hospital. Scarcely had he begun his training when the outbreak of a cholera epidemic threw all routine into disarray as help was urgently needed to tend the stricken and dying all around. An estimated sixty-five percent of those who died in the outbreak were from the East End slums. Barnardo gave his time and strength in unstinting self-sacrifice to bring relief wherever he could, even though he was forced to witness sights so grievous that he could never fully erase them from his memory.

As the epidemic died down, Barnardo began his medical studies in earnest. But he still found time to teach in the Ernest Street School, preach at street corners, and search out the outcast and drifting with the gospel of the grace of God. No drinking house or gambling den was too rough or too evil for the dauntless evangelist to venture. His unconventional methods, coupled with his deep pity for the broken and drifting humanity all around him, won for Barnardo a hearing where others could gain no entrance.

One evening he followed a group of enthusiastic youngsters as they entered an establishment equivalent to a modern amusement arcade to gamble away their pittance of money. Angered at such exploitation, he asked the proprietor if he might address a few words to the lads. Suspecting his motives, the proprietor demanded a fee of £5 before giving permission – an exorbitant price for those days. As he handed over half the money, Barnardo also laid down a condition: that he was to speak without interruption. Rising to address the young people, he was greeted with boos and jeers for many of them recognised him from his street corner preaching. Unexpectedly Barnardo offered to sing them a song if they would be quiet. Arrested by such an approach, these rough boys listened in silence as Barnardo finished his song and then began to point out the evils of the place they were in and speak of the lasting treasures to be found in the gospel.

This was too much for the proprietor, who broke his terms of the contract by interrupting the preacher and insisting that he clear off the premises. Reclaiming his money, Barnardo left the hall declaring, 'My lads, I am not allowed to finish, but if you care to listen I shall be outside the front.' Like another Pied Piper, Barnardo discovered the hall emptying rapidly as he retreated, and soon all the young people were gathered in front of him outside as he continued his sermon from the eminence of a costermonger's barrow. 'Thank you,' 'God bless you,' 'We wish you would come again,' many of these youngsters called out as Barnardo took his leave.

Barnardo was becoming a familiar figure in some of the worst East End areas, so placing himself at considerable risk. One evening as he rose to preach at a cottage meeting in a particularly rough district of Stepney a gang of semi-drunken youths planned to assault him while he was preaching. Half filling the room, the gang only awaited a signal from their leader, a local 'bruiser', to begin the assault. Impatiently they watched but still the signal did not come.

'Hey, bruiser, what abart th' fun?' cried one gang member in annoyance. But the 'bruiser' could not take his eyes off the preacher's face. For there, addressing the meeting, was the very man who had risked his life to care for him when he had lain critically ill with cholera. Turning to his increasingly restless confederates, the gang leader exclaimed, 'If any o' you chaps touches this man, you settles wi' me!' And before the meeting had closed this needy young man had asked Barnardo to pray for him. For hours through the night he struggled to find the peace with God he now earnestly sought. With Barnardo's help he at last experienced the joy of knowing himself a forgiven man for Christ's sake. William Notman was to become one of Barnardo's most valued fellow workers in years to come.

But not always did Barnardo's encounters with the tough and hardened youths of the London streets end in such a way. On another occasion he found himself in 'a long, low, narrow den crowded with lads and girls', most of whom were the worse for drink. He had come to sell copies of the Scriptures, but even the offer of a song could not tame this mob. After many attempts to make himself master of the situation, Barnardo was eventually flung down from the table on which he was standing. Several of the most drunken youths placed the table upside down on the prostrate man and began dancing a tattoo on top of him. Unconscious, badly bruised and with several broken ribs, Barnardo was eventually carried back to his accommodation. But penitent for their ribaldry and drunken violence, the leaders of the gang visited Barnardo every day during his convalescence to enquire about his recovery. Many were the conversations he held with them, and in his judgment, this incident gained him a hearing with these youths not possible otherwise.

Such incidents as these were typical of Barnardo's unique approach. But his individuality, enthusiasm and innovations did not always endear him to other conscientious Christians who disagreed with some of his unusual methods. The ideas he wished to put into practice at the Ernest Street School often left the existing staff bemused and not a little exasperated. They preferred the more conventional ways they had always used, yet could not deny the magnetic power of Barnardo's personality over the very children and young people whom they most wished to help. So while still seeking to work harmoniously with the school, Tom Barnardo decided that the best solution would be to start a 'ragged' school of his own. Ensuring that the hours of the two schools would not clash, Barnardo set out to look for suitable premises.

At last he discovered a derelict barn, currently used as a donkey shed. This the enterprising young medical student hired for a small rent. And here, with the help of some student friends, the inhospitable barn was prepared for its new use. They covered the earth floor, whitewashed the walls and ceiling and repaired the broken fireplace. Advertising his school, Barnardo quickly gathered into the transformed shed many of the area's destitute and aimless children. Unwittingly he had set out on a path that was leading him onward to the life work God had prepared for him.

Barnardo's days were crammed with activity: Bible training, medical studies, street preaching, and teaching both at the Ernest Street School and, of course, in his own school which was situated in an alleyway appropriately known as Hope Place. And into the Hope Place school one bitterly cold day in the winter of 1866 slipped a sorry little figure. The ten-year old, clad only in filthy and inadequate rags, wormed his way to the fire, and there sat mesmerised by the flickering flames. As darkness began to gather Barnardo dismissed the children and then started to close up the barn-school for the night. Just as he was about to bolt the doors he saw the child, lying on the floor half hidden by the box on which he had previously been sitting.

'Here, my lad,' he remonstrated sharply, 'wake up, and off home to your mother!'

'Ain't got no mother, sir,' came the pitiful reply.

'Well, then, off to your father.'

'Got no father neither, sir,' retorted the lad.

'Away then to your home, wherever it is,' said Barnardo.

'Oi've got no 'ome, sir . . . Oi – don't – live – nowhere.'

Though wise to the pranks of little East Enders, Barnardo sensed that this ragged urchin could be speaking the truth.

But was it possible that so young a child could be sleeping rough in the depths of winter? As he drew the little boy into the circle of light cast by the gas lamp, Barnardo realised that here was a case needing urgent investigation. With bare arms and legs, with neither shirt nor underclothing and only short ragged trousers covering his wasted and dirty body, the child had awakened Barnardo's deepest pity. He looked more like a seven-year-old than a boy of ten; and later he was to describe the neglected little chap, whose name he discovered was Jim Jarvis, in these words: 'His face was not the face of a child. It bore a careworn, old-mannish look, only relieved by the bright keen glances of his small sharp eyes.' He looked 'sadly overwise' and spoke in 'querulous high-pitched tones'. Either Jim was a cunning little liar, or Barnardo had stumbled on one of the most crying social evils imaginable – worse than anything he had previously encountered.

'Tell me, my lad, are there other poor boys like you in London without home or friends?' enquired Barnardo

A grim smile lit up Jim's grubby face. 'Oh yes, sir, lots – 'eaps of 'em; more'n oi could count!' Clearly this was either a child's fabrication or a situation requiring his urgent attention. Barnardo thought quickly.

'Now Jim, if I give you some hot coffee and a place to sleep in will you take me to where some of these poor boys are, as you say, lying out in the streets?'

'That oi will, sir, and no mistake,' was the boy's sturdy response.

Over coffee and sandwiches Jim told his story, and a pathetic one it was: his father he had never even heard spoken of; his mother had died some years earlier and Jim had been taken to a workhouse. So unhappy was he there that he had eventually run away, only to become a virtual slave of a drunken bargeman known as Swearin' Dick. Beaten mercilessly by his employer, the child had run away once more and now daily wandered the London streets, 'pickin' up what he cu'd'.

Not content with feeding Jim, Barnardo spoke to the boy in the simplest terms of the compassion of the Son of God who too had been beaten, abused by callous men and crowned with thorns. Tears began to trickle down Jim's grubby face as he listened to all his benefactor told him. But when he heard of the crucifixion of Jesus Christ, Jim began to sob, 'Oh sir,' he exclaimed through his tears, 'that wor wuss than Swearin' Dick sarved me!'

By now it was long after midnight. After praying with Jim, Barnardo took the child's hand and together they set off to find the scores of other young boys whom Jim assured him were in a similar plight. Down narrow lanes and dark alleyways they walked until at last they reached a dead end with a wall cutting off any further progress. There Jim stopped and said, 'Up there, sir!' Barnardo could see nothing. Perhaps it was all a hoax after all. Then he realised that Jim was indicating that he must scale the ten-foot wall. Scrambling up himself by means of fingerholds and footholds in the crumbling bricks, Jim disappeared from sight. After a moment or two he reappeared with a stick which he held out to help Barnardo to ascend. Once up, a sight met his eyes that left him dumbfounded:

There, with their heads upon the higher part, and their feet somewhat in the gutter, but in a great variety of postures lay a confused heap of boys on an open roof – all asleep. I counted eleven. No covering of any kind was upon them. The rags they wore were mere apologies for clothes . . . as bad as, if not worse than Jim's. One big fellow who lay there seemed about eighteen; the ages of the remainder varied, I should say, from nine to fourteen.

As Barnardo gazed at the sleeping children the moon came out from behind a cloud, casting its pale light across their faces. 'It was as though the hand of God himself had suddenly pulled aside the curtain' and shown him 'the untold miseries of forlorn child-life upon the streets of London'. The sight of those 'upturned faces white with cold and hunger' was to haunt him for many weeks to come.

'Shall we go to another lay, sir? *There's lots more!*' Jim was tugging impatiently at his coat. But Tom Barnardo had seen enough for one night. China at that moment seemed remote indeed, and the needs of outcast children very close at hand.

Barnardo's horror at the plight of these homeless urchins gradually gave way to a determination to help. But what could he do? Only a medical student, he was dependent on finance from his father to cover his personal expenses. First, however, he must make some arrangement for Jim. This he did by allowing him to sleep in his own accommodation until a kindly family agreed to clothe and house the boy. Then he had to discover the truth behind Jim's assertion that there were *lots more* places, *'eaps of 'em*, where homeless children found shelter at night. With Jim's help, Barnardo did indeed discover scores of hideouts – 'lays', as Jim had called them – where such pathetic outcasts gathered.

Everywhere Barnardo went he spoke of this appalling need in an attempt to rouse the conscience of the Christian public to the destitution so near at hand. Early in 1867 a quite unexpected opportunity arose for Barnardo to do this very thing. A large gathering at the Agricultural Hall in London had been convened to stimulate interest in foreign missions and, as a missionary candidate, Barnardo was invited to occupy a seat on the platform. But the main speaker appeared to have been delayed. Moments ticked by and still he had not come. As the time to open the meeting arrived, the vast congregation began to grow restless. Then a note was delivered to the anxious chairman to say that the speaker had been taken ill and would be unable to fulfil his engagement. With a surge of desperation, the chairman cast round for an alternative speaker. His eyes alighted on the small bespectacled figure on the platform. Had not this youth just been telling him of the plight of London's homeless children? Surely this was a form of missionary work. So the unprepared young man was asked to address the audience – an endless sea of faces spread out before him in row after row. With a silent prayer for God's special help, Tom Barnardo rose to speak. For more than an hour the company listened with riveted attention as he told the grievous story of all he had discovered in recent weeks.

Among those particularly moved that night was a servant girl who pressed forward and thrust a bag of farthings into Barnardo's hands. 'To help the poor waifs on London's streets,' she said simply, adding that she wanted him to use the money – her entire savings – for that purpose. Before he could learn the girl's name, she had disappeared into the crowd. Barnardo now found himself custodian of the first sum of money given to help the children of London , twenty-seven farthings in all – little enough in man's sight, but precious in the eyes of God.

His unexpected Agricultural Hall address had other far-reaching consequences. Reported in the press, it evoked strong reactions: some censured it bitterly, while others joined in the clamour of demand that immediate action be taken to address such a situation. Among those who followed the correspondence with concern was none other than Lord Shaftesbury. Known as 'the Good Earl', Shaftesbury had long been a benefactor of the downtrodden and underprivileged. A former member of Parliament for Woodstock, he had spearheaded the reform of the Poor Laws. Now as a member of the House of Lords he continued to guide legislation through the Upper House for the improvement of conditions for the poverty-stricken masses. As chairman of the 'Ragged School Union' and champion of education for the children of the poor, he found Barnardo's revelations deeply disturbing.

While others accused Barnardo of exaggeration and even deliberate deception, Shaftesbury remained silent, knowing enough of the social evils prevalent in the capital to wish to investigate for himself. Summoning Barnardo to his office, he arranged for a debate between some of Barnardo's critics and the outspoken missionary candidate. Searching questions, often hostile, were posed. For each Barnardo had a ready answer. At last came the Earl's final challenge: 'If these statements are true, will you pilot us into the East End and show us the sights described?' Willingly he would, answered Barnardo, with the same confidence Jim had earlier displayed. Another opportunity might be difficult to organise, so why not investigate that very night?

Leading the well-heeled group through endless alleyways and streets fouled with household rubbish, Barnardo hoped fervently that he might find some significant 'lay' of homeless children. A cutting wind repeatedly blew out the matches with which they tried to cast some light on the upturned boxes and barrels that might be roof and bed for some destitute child. Sceptical whispers began to be exchanged as the hunt went on. Unwilling to acknowledge defeat, Barnardo was searching a large area covered by a tarpaulin. Constantly he thrust his arm down under it, groping after some child's hands or feet. Again and again he found nothing.

Then he began investigating in a place where two tarpaulins overlapped. Suddenly he felt a foot. Grabbing it firmly, he pulled until first a body and then the face of a half-starved boy appeared. Imagining he had been caught by the police, the child began to whimper. But on the assurance that he was among friends, and with the encouragement of a small bribe, he willingly turned guide and soon led the party to an area of the tarpaulin that began to heave with human life as blinking and sleepy boys were dragged from their lair. At last seventy-three children had been discovered, aged between seven and seventeen – all clad only in rotting and evil-smelling rags. Here was proof enough that Tom Barnardo had spoken the sober truth. Leading the homeless army to a nearby café, still open, Shaftesbury ordered them all to eat until they could eat no more, and he would pay the bill.

Now three o'clock in the morning, the boys were dismissed with the promise of further help, and the party turned wearily homeward. But before they left Shaftesbury drew Barnardo aside. Apologising for those who had cast doubt on his word, he said, 'I thank God, sir, for your work! These children must be saved from the horrors of their lot. You hope to go as a missionary to China. That is a noble ambition; God needs many labourers in China. But pray earnestly over the events of this night. It may be that God is calling you to labour as his chosen missionary among the homeless children of this Metropolis.'

As Barnardo turned over in his mind all that had taken place that night, it became clear to him that God had been directing his way. At best he had hoped to discover a dozen or so children sleeping rough, but to find over seventy in such a condition was significant in a number of ways. First, it more than vindicated his words before a Victorian public, in general unprepared to recognise the evils existing all around them. More than this, it gained for him the support of one of England's most influential politicians. And most importantly, it engraved the needs of the abused and destitute children of the East End of London indelibly on his heart for ever. The words of the Earl of Shaftesbury, too, had a profound effect on the young man as he increasingly began to identify in them the voice of God calling him out to a service far other than he had anticipated.

Ever a dreamer of great and sometimes impossible dreams, Barnardo began to plan ways in which he could help these children, both spiritually and physically. His first action was to send out letters urgently requesting donations for his efforts. Next he decided to rent rooms to accommode both his Hope Place school during the week and Sunday services especially designed for the outcast children and un- churched young adults of the area. He would need not only dedicated Christians to join him in such endeavour but considerable financial backing. Both requirements he found difficult to meet. But regardless of discouragements, he rented premises known as the Assembly Rooms, situated above the King's Arms, a public house in Mile End Road. On 5 November 1867, having arrived in London only eighteen months, before, Tom Barnardo opened the Rooms with a free tea, attracting 'no less than 2,347 rough lads, young men, girls, and young women, a large proportion of the older ones being thieves and poor lost girls.' Rough indeed they were, and 'the noise and the tumult were terrible' making it nearly impossible for the earnest evangelist to make his voice heard above the racket when he attempted to address them. But it was at least a beginning, and for six weeks the people poured into the Assembly Rooms.

But when Barnardo and his helpers arrived one Sunday morning to open up the premises, he discovered the place barred against him and the landlord, who was also the proprietor of the King's Arms, adamant that on no account would Barnardo and his helpers be allowed any further use of the premises. Not only did he disapprove of the type of people gathering above his public house, but in addition, his trade was beginning to suffer as the message Barnardo proclaimed was transforming the lives of his erstwhile customers.

Even with his effervescent personality, this reverse had a crushing effect on Barnardo's spirits. So certain had he been of God's leading that he was deeply perplexed at the turn of events. But only a week later he was taken ill with an infection that brought all his activities to a standstill for two months. With no-one to oversee his work effectively, it would have had to be closed down in any case. As Barnardo recognised the providence behind these circumstances, he utilised the long weeks of convalescence in planning for the future. From his sick bed he encouraged his friends to rent a small room from which a nucleus of the work could be carried on. By March the following year he was well enough to rent two small houses back in Hope Place. One for boys and the other for girls; these houses were to be open continually, not only as a ragged school, but for a number of social activities: a sewing room, a lending library, evening classes, prayer meetings and, of course, Sunday services and teaching activities. An ambitious programme, Barnardo dubbed it *The East End Juvenile Mission.*

Meanwhile Barnardo was also tackling the problem of homelessness by finding Christian families where some of the neediest children could be cared for. But many of the boys were hardened little rogues who had been on the streets for so long that they were not amenable to the disciplines of normal home life. No other solution could he find but to allow them to sleep in the cottages in Hope Place, so placing them under a strict and ever-watchful regime of controls. From this small seed was to spring up the mighty organisation reaching world-wide forever associated with the name of Tom Barnardo – a development described as 'without parallel in the history of benevolent achievement'.

Still a medical student at the London Hospital and only twenty-four years of age, Barnardo's two cottages soon become four as he rented adjacent houses that became available. Yet never did Barnardo lose sight of the spiritual objectives of his work. Services were held each Sunday afternoon in the largest room available – one seating up to seventy people. Barnardo himself would stand on the stairs so that his voice could be heard in all the nearby rooms, and many were the converts of his urgent gospel preaching during those days. When a larger assembly room was needed for the Sunday gatherings, they demolished the intersecting walls of the rear yards of the four cottages and threw a roof over the whole area, so obtaining a hall large enough to seat three hundred.

And still the burgeoning work made additional premises imperative. Then it was that Tom Barnardo obtained the leasehold of a large property at 18 Stepney Causeway. Now at last he could see his way clear to bringing many destitute boys together under one roof. Sixty could be accommodated in five dormitories in the new premises; but his vision was yet more comprehensive. Boys with homes but no work were also to be enrolled for training in basic working skills at Number 18, while lads from better backgrounds, whose parents could contribute financially towards the home, were admitted to the training schemes.

Recreation too was to be provided and a timetable established to include morning and evening prayers, two periods of academic work, a period of industrial training, open air sports, time for reading and meditation, and three meals each day. Considerable finance was required and never at this stage of his work would Barnardo proceed with any development until all expenses were met. Relying implicitly on a covenant-honouring and prayer-hearing God, he saw constant and indubitable evidences that all his needs were known on high and met through the loving and generous gifts of Christian people.

When 18, Stepney Causeway was leased to Barnardo, he was also given the option to lease the adjoining premises if need should arise. And a wise provision it proved. One biting winter's day, not long after the Stepney Causeway home had become fully operational, a child of eleven, his face pinched with hunger and cold and clad only in ragged trousers, appeared at the door and begged for admission. Carrots – for so the other street boys had dubbed the freckle-faced youngster – told Barnardo a heart-breaking story. His mother, a gin addict, had turned him onto the streets when he was seven. Never again did he see her except when she caught him near his home, and then she would rifle his pockets for money to finance her addiction. Barnardo listened sadly, but though he yearned to help the child, the home was full and he could only give him a hot meal and some money in his pocket and promise that if he returned in a week's time there would be room for him. In the bitterly cold days that followed, Carrots was unable to sell any matches to earn his scrap of food. Before the week was out, as two Billingsgate workmen upturned a disused beer barrel, they discovered a thin freckle-faced boy underneath, apparently asleep. But Carrots was dead.

An inquest passed the verdict: 'Death from exhaustion, the result of frequent exposure and want of food.' Barnardo was inconsolable. He blamed himself for the child's death. If only he had taken him in when he had come to his door the previous week. But as a result of this tragedy he made a new resolution. With God's help, never again would he turn away a destitute child. Acting on his resolution, he had a sign made which read: NO DESTITUTE CHILD EVER REFUSED ADMISSION. This he erected over the entrance of the Stepney Causeway home. In this act of daring faith, Barnardo was cast upon his God in a new way, for the need, as he well knew, could place upon him demands beyond anything he could hope to meet.

Number 18 soon overflowed into Number 20, and to these were added 22, 24 and 26. Before the 1870s were out, the whole block constituted the first Barnardo Homes. And as if this was not enough to pacify Barnardo's insatiable urge to serve his God with all his strength, during the same period, he opened more than a dozen further centres for daytime training among disadvantaged children and adults. The most significant and daring of these schemes was the purchase of *The Edinburgh Castle*.

These were days when God was blessing his church mightily. Following the outpouring of the Spirit in 1859 in Ireland and many other parts of the British Isles, evangelistic efforts were unusually successful. With the co-operation of his helpers in the newly-fledged *East London Juvenile Mission*, Barnardo invited an evangelist, Joshua Poole, and his wife, Mary, to hold a Tent Mission in the East End. The tent, seating 3,000, was pitched outside one of the largest and vilest 'gin-palaces' in the area, an edifice known as *The Edinburgh Castle*. Well-lit with a glittering frontage, this drinking house was built like a castle complete with turrets and a flagpole, and was decorated inside with mirrors, flashing lights and nude statues. Known for its loud music and bawdy jokes, the Castle kept up a nefarious trade, selling quantities of gin to its customers, many of whom were as addicted as Carrots' mother.

But the tent mission changed all that. Barnardo describes one particular evening:

The scenes we are permitted to witness nightly are such as I never remember beholding during any previous period of my spiritual life. Last Lord's Day evening twenty-five hundred persons crowded to hear the Word of Life, and for hours afterwards we were occupied in dealing with anxious souls.

Linked with any profession of faith, Barnardo encouraged converts to take a temperance pledge, for he had witnessed the devastating effects of alcohol on the impoverished East End communities.

As a direct result of the tent mission, *The Edinburgh Castle* lost a large proportion of its customers and soon came on the market for sale. Barnardo eyed the building with longing. If the people were being encouraged to give up their drinking habits, why not turn the magnificent edifice into a 'coffee palace' and a centre for Christian work? Writing to his friends and supporters, Barnardo described the facilities: 'a splendid house, containing eighteen rooms; a large well-ventilated apartment seating 200 persons; another great concert room with seats for 1,100; and grounds surrounding the same sufficiently large to enable us, if necessary, to hold tent services . . . '

Soon the money began to come in, but time was at a premium, for on 22 October 1872 the great building was due to come up for auction. Interest was keen, and a number of other organisations saw the potential of *The Edinburgh Castle*. Fearful of losing a prize of such potential for the kingdom of God, Tom Barnardo knew that he must buy the building outright by private contract. He offered £4,200 for it only one hour before it was due to be auctioned. Individual gifts from such philanthropists as Lord Radstock and Lord Shaftesbury defrayed the larger part of the cost.

Out went the statues and all the trappings of the *Castle's* past disreputable trade. But Barnardo foresaw (unusually for a Victorian) that the bright decor, chandeliers and mirrors could attract the working man. These therefore would remain. The palace was then attractively decorated throughout, with Scripture texts and tasteful pictures. Here in the *Edinburgh Castle People's Mission Church* cheap meals would be served, papers and magazines sold, games facilities provided, and regular Sunday services conducted.

Opened by Lord Shaftesbury himself in February 1873, the venture was a success from the beginning. The people poured in. Barnardo himself, highly gifted as a preacher, took the services two or three times each week with numbers often exceeding 3,000. Ten years later the overcrowding made the erection of a new hall essential. His friends begged him to give up his charitable work and become the full time pastor of the Castle Church, but Barnardo could never agree. 'I feel my Master has called me and given me as a life-work my children,' he said simply, '*and for nothing can I desert them.*'

Throughout this period Barnardo continued his medical studies. But something else was playing on his mind. Struggle as he might he could not banish from his thoughts a young lady whom he had met briefly on two occasions in 1871. Syrie Elmslie, only daughter of a wealthy city businessman, figured constantly in both his daytime thoughts and in his dreams. Brought up in a comfortable environment, worldly and irreligious, Syrie had had little time for God until at eighteen she had come under the preaching of Lord Radstock. This had altered her thinking and life for ever. Truly converted to God, Syrie had then thrown all her time and energies into charitable work, which had led to one or two fleeting encounters with Tom Barnardo. But for eighteen months neither had seen the other until they chanced to meet when both were attending the funeral of a well-known Christian.

Not given to procrastination once he had made up his mind on a project, Barnardo offered to escort Syrie back to her accommodation. Declaring his affection and finding it reciprocated, he arranged without delay to visit her family home in Richmond to ask for Syrie's hand in marriage. When he arrived at Richmond station three days later he found a cab waiting to take him to the home. Climbing into the cab, he enquired whether the 'nice little lad' seated beside the cabman was the cabman's son. In fact it was Syrie's younger brother. Despite this *faux pas*, permission was granted to the eager trainee doctor and child benefactor to marry Syrie. Four weeks later, in the spring of 1873, the wedding service was conducted at the Metropolitan Tabernacle and attended by capacity crowds. In the absence of Spurgeon himself, Dr Grattan Guinness, Barnardo's longstanding friend, officiated at the ceremony.

Even on his honeymoon Barnardo was thinking and planning further ways to rescue destitute and needy children. So far he had been able to help only boys, but the plight of homeless girls was equally, if not more desperate. Frequently as he visited lodging houses he found little girls abused and exploited, with many as young as thirteen or fourteen, struggling on their own to cope with babies. Suicide and neglect or even murder of their babies were not uncommon.

Soon after returning from honeymoon, Barnardo and his wife received the gift of a small estate in Barkingside, Essex, expressly donated to serve both as their own home and as accommodation for needy girls. By the autumn of 1873 the first twelve girls were received at Mossford Lodge, and within a year Syrie and Tom Barnardo had more than fifty girls under their roof. But the scheme was not a success. Vile conversation overheard amongst the girls, coupled with actions that reflected the evil surroundings from which they had been rescued, made Barnardo realise that these girls needed to be handled in a different way from the boys.

Deeply troubled one night by the depraved conduct he discovered among some of 'his' girls, many already hardened and cynical, Barnardo had a strange dream. He saw in his dream a delightful country cottage – ivy creeping up the walls and flowers brightening the garden. Looking through the lighted window, he saw a dozen or more girls clustered around a kindly-looking woman who was reading to them from the Bible, and as he listened he heard her read words from Psalm 68, 'He setteth the solitary in families.' Then in his dream Barnardo looked more closely at the faces of the girls in the cottage. To his astonishment he recognised each as one of his 'own' girls. 'Syrie, Syrie,'

Barnardo called out, waking his wife, 'it has been revealed to me how to deal with our girls!'

Attending a conference a few days later he confided his ideas to a friend. The next morning a total stranger offered to build the first cottage in the 'girls' village' in memory of a child he had lost. By the following summer foundation stones were laid for a further thirteen cottages and also of a laundry building. In accordance with his dream, each cottage housed between twelve and fifteen girls, with a cottage mother to care for the 'family'. By the time of Barnardo's death almost thirty years later, over seventy cottages clustered around lawns and gardens in that village estate in Barkingside. Twenty-four thousand girls had been rescued from a life of exploitation and vice, many of them given a home in the village, clothed, educated, trained and employed.

In March 1876 Barnardo finally sat and passed his medical examinations, graduating as a licentiate of the Royal College of Surgeons. Happily married and with his work among destitute children progressing on all fronts, Barnardo was nevertheless about to face the fiercest trial of his life. A natural leader and innovator, Barnardo had won many friends and admirers. But like other men of vision and determination, he could often be dictatorial in his ways, causing others to be either jealous of his success or in strong disagreement with his unconventional methods. Among the former employees of Barnardo's institutions were also malcontents who had been dismissed over the years for a variety of reasons. A number of these people were on the alert to find fault with Barnardo and his organisations.

In certain areas he was unquestionably vulnerable to hostile criticism. Unwisely Barnardo had personally handled all the funds donated over the years from thousands of Christians and other charities towards his work. A mere

£200 in 1867 had swelled to an astonishing £20,000 a year in 1876. With none to oversee his accounts, he was wide open to accusations of making fraudulent appeals and embezzlement of funds.

The first whisper of trouble came from a series of anonymous letters to Syrie, accusing her husband of unnamed but serious misconduct. Barnardo too received such letters implicating his wife in deceitful and underhand behaviour. Worse was to follow. The rumours increased: not only was he guilty of embezzlement, but he was half-starving and maltreating children in his care. Some were kept in underground cells, damp and rat infested; others were severely beaten, the doors of their rooms nailed shut for many days at a time. As the weeks passed the rumours grew yet more lurid. Rats bit the children's toes, mud oozed from the floors of their rooms, and Barnardo himself was 'a wolf in sheep's clothing'.

Stung to the quick by such monstrous accusations, Barnardo allowed a friend to write an anonymous letter to the press ostensibly to vindicate him. But the indiscretions of this hot-headed friend aggravated the situation yet further. And when he wrote a second letter with added inflammatory salvos, Barnardo was appalled – and even more so when he himself was accused of being the secret author of these letters.

Trouble seemed to threaten his work on every hand. Next a booklet appeared entitled, *Dr Barnardo's Homes: Containing Startling Revelations*. This publication listed a catalogue of charges and innuendoes, damaging in the extreme, not only to Barnardo's work amongst children but also to his own character as a moral and upright Christian man. Vitriolic and suggestive accusations appeared on every page, tearing this large-hearted man's character to shreds. Christians were now becoming bemused, puzzled and suspicious. Perhaps there was truth in these accusations.

The Charity Organisation Society, which monitored all institutions like Barnardo's homes, put his work on their cautionary list, pending a full investigation.

Although Barnardo might have wished to ignore the accusations, hoping that in time he would be vindicated, it now became plain that every avenue of his work must be investigated in order to set the minds of generous Christian supporters at rest. An arbitration board was therefore set up, consisting of a panel of three, impartial and disinterested in their judgments: a QC, a minister of religion, and an ex-MP, none of whom had previously been linked in any way to Barnardo's cause. Several prominent judges, represented each side of the divide. The board sat for almost forty working days, carefully examining each accusation in turn, together with every aspect of the daily running of the homes. Meanwhile a firm of chartered accountants examined the finances in detail. A further two months were then to elapse while the board prepared to present its findings – months of stressful anxiety for Barnardo.

At last, on 15 October 1877, the three arbitrators were ready to deliver the results of the investigations – a ten-thousand word document, personally signed by all three. 'The Barnardo Institutions,' it pronounced, were 'real and valuable charities, worthy of public confidence and support.' The charge of misappropriation of funds was discovered to be entirely without foundation, with the handling of money committed to Barnardo marked by 'thorough efficiency'. The general management of the homes was declared to be 'judicious', and no evidence at all could be found to support the accusations of cruelty or unsatisfactory conditions. Of great importance, the arbitrators declared the personal attacks on Barnardo's character to be 'gossip of the most malignant sort'.

Relieved and vindicated, Barnardo was now free to carry on his work. But the repercussions of the inquiry for the child rescue programme to which he had dedicated his life, enabled him to recognise a hidden providence behind the trial, for the controversy had brought the homes to public attention in an unprecedented way. The press, which had reported and inflamed the accusations, now extensively detailed the results of the arbitration. Whereas his work had formerly been known to a relatively small circle, 'Barnardo's' now became a familiar word throughout the land. Barnardo himself had been catapulted to fame and was recognised far and wide as a national asset, the friend of the outcast and needy.

But more than this: although thoroughly vindicating Barnardo, the arbitration board, made certain recommendations. His educational establishments ought to come under government inspection and so become eligible for government grants. A committee should be appointed to manage all aspects of the Homes and the finances should be administered by a board and inspected regularly by independent financiers. All these decisions were wise and Barnardo readily complied with them. The management of the organisations which he had instituted had now grown far beyond the capacity of any single individual to direct in a satisfactory manner.

Criticisms did not vanish overnight, but they were now muted and widely recognised as the cavillings of jealous and bitter individuals. Even in our own day, nearly a hundred years after the death of Dr Barnardo, unjust and ill-founded accusations have again been voiced and reported in the media against the character and methods employed by this honourable Christian. Many of these criticisms are anachronistic in character, judging nineteenth-century conditions by today's welfare guidelines. But as in the 1870s, such censures can still often be traced to the religious and ethical stance of those who initiate them.

In any outline of the triumphs, struggles, sorrows and enterprises of Dr Barnardo's life, it would be impossible to cover adequately the extraordinary developments of his work during the twenty-eight years that remained to him after these events. A report that he himself compiled in 1888, detailing the progress of his work since the arbitration eleven years earlier, demonstrates the astonishing increases on all fronts in that period. Whereas 2,000 children had been rescued from a life of destitution in the eleven years up to 1877, now he could record that 12,653 had been housed clothed, educated and employed. At this stage Barnardo tried wherever possible to place younger boys in the care of foster parents and only bring them into the various homes as they entered their teenage years to receive a training which would enable them to earn a living. Up until 1878 Barnardo's work had consisted of eight separate institutions, with fourteen cottages in the Girls' Village Home. Now, eleven years later, thirty-eight distinct branches of the work had been established, with fifty homes built in the Girls' Village and a further nineteen under construction. Not far away a similar enterprise known as the Boys' Garden City was housing an increasing number of boys in similar 'family' units.

Barnardo was also troubled by the needs of neglected infants. Night after night as he combed the streets or answered appeals for help he discovered sick, unwanted and orphaned babies. Sometimes the mother had died in childbirth. Other babies had mothers who were either feckless and negligent, unable to provide roof or food, or simply too sick or poor to care for their infants. Barnardo preferred to have babies or toddlers who were in reasonable health fostered in the home of some kindly Christians. But a destitute, undernourished and ailing baby needing special care would be taken to the 'Babies' Castle' in Hawkhurst, Kent. There amid lovely surroundings as many as seventy babies at a time were cared for by trained nurses before being assigned to foster homes.

Barnardo's policy of placing many girls into service in countries such as Canada and Australia has come under recent criticism. To remove a child from everything she had previously known, placing an ocean between her homeland and her new environment, has been regarded as questionable if not cruel. But Barnardo himself defended the practice by pointing out that girls had a far greater chance of leading a life of successful employment in Canada than in England. Most were delighted to go and settled well.

Many boys also were given opportunities abroad, some in farming, some in industry, while others trained for life in the marines. For the younger children who went abroad, homes were carefully selected in country areas so give these youngsters opportunities of childhood joys which would be forever denied them had they remained or returned to the sordid environment from which they had been rescued. The evident success of these schemes can be judged from the enthusiastic letters and generous donations which many children sent back to the Barnardo Homes as they received their regular pay packets in their new countries.

Never did Barnardo allow his tireless efforts for the social relief of boys and girls to disturb his spiritual priorities. Only a deep and inward work of God in the souls of the children in his care could bring about permanent good. Mercurial and cheerful by temperament, he yet warned the children of the sinfulness of sin in the sight of God, together with the devastation it could bring into their lives. When a party of boys and girls was about to emigrate, he would address them, urging them to hold fast to the Word of God, prayer, a good conscience, and to seek a living relationship with the Saviour.

In their own lives together Tom and Syrie Barnardo experienced deep personal sorrows. Three out of their five sons died while young. Nine-year-old Herbert's death pierced through his father's heart like a sword. Yet as he cradled his dying boy, he was the more confirmed in his God-given task. Later he wrote:

As I gazed into the little pinched face, growing cold in death, hundreds of other child faces appeared to me through his, while other wistful eyes looked out at me by the waning light of his dear eyes . . . I dare not turn aside from this work. By God's help I will not.

When Kennie, a boy of remarkable intelligence and attractive personality, also died it seemed to the broken-hearted parents a grief almost too hard to be borne. But as his coffin was being carried to Bow Cemetery, the funeral procession passed the coffin of an East End child also about to be buried. No flowers adorned that stark little coffin. With a surge of compassion Barnardo took two wreathes off Kennie's coffin and said simply to the bereaved parents, 'From my child to yours.'

A man of tireless energy, Barnardo seemed to need less sleep than most. Frequent nights would be spent in search of needy children, and there were few lodging houses where Barnardo's face was unknown. On occasions he had even joined the inmates, experiencing for himself the appalling conditions of filth, vermin and infestation – the common lot of many young boys lucky enough to have a bed to lie on. During the forty years of his rescue work it is doubtful whether he ever had more than six hours of sleep at night.

Barnardo's dedication inspired a similar devotion among the hundreds of men and women who worked with him in the Homes. 'I doubt if ever there lived a man possessed of greater genius for inspiring in his associates the desire to do only their best,' said one who had worked closely with Barnardo for many years. His ability to discern character and aptitude in the staff he employed prevented much disharmony. But even Barnardo could make mistakes.

Writing of one house mother who had the care of sick children, he complained in a letter to Syrie, 'Sister M. does not care one atom for them. She has never kissed a child since she came. She has no heart for the poor dears. . .'

But the cost of his incessant toil was high, and by the time Barnardo was fifty his health had begun to break. When a heart condition was diagnosed, his doctor warned him severely against his life style. But the daily demands of his work spoke more loudly than the doctor's warnings. Six or seven minor heart attacks followed in the next ten years, but still this tireless man laboured on, knowing that his days could well be numbered. One of his last letters written to a bereaved friend expressed his outlook:

I have looked into the face of death. Three times has my life been given back to me. . . But Oh! I can tell you, Death to the Christian is not so dark as it is painted. I felt as in the embrace of a friend.

And as he made out his will he wrote:

Death and the Grave are but temporary bonds; Christ has triumphed over them! I hope to die as I have lived, in the humble but assured faith of Jesus Christ, whom I have so imperfectly served, and whom I acknowledge to be my Saviour, Master and King.

In 1905, not long after his sixtieth birthday, Barnardo suffered a further severe attack of angina. The end seemed imminent. 'Oh Syrie! My head feels so heavy,' he exclaimed, as he lay against her, struggling for breath. And in moments this great champion of outcast children had passed beyond those sickening sights of sorrow and destitution he had striven so hard to remedy. The trumpets had sounded once more.

Such scenes of public grief following Barnardo's death, the East End of London had rarely witnessed before. Never, said representatives of one national newspaper, had there been such a funeral since that of Queen Victoria herself four years earlier. All traffic for more than three miles came to a standstill as thousands thronged to see the cortege pass – the stillness broken only by the audible sobs of those who had loved the Doctor and whose children had been rescued and transformed by his vision and initiative. Even the newspaper boys had pooled their meagre resources to buy wreathes for the coffin.

Tributes from all over the world flooded in, with the press in every English speaking country carrying extensive records of his life and achievements. And well they might, for over 60,000 children had passed through Barnardo's homes and agencies by that time. A London paper wrote, 'He passed with silent steps through reeking slums, like some good angel sent by Grace Divine, and stretched a helping hand to helpless infancy, throwing the mantle of boundless charity around the crouching figures of the homeless poor. The man was great . . . his lofty soul reached beyond the bounds of nationhood, girding the world with love.' More personal was the tribute of his old friend Henry Grattan Guinness, whose own grief ran deep:

Beloved Dr Barnardo with his beaming face, cheery voice, broad brow, big brain, glowing heart, indomitable courage, tender sympathy, intense philanthropy, unwearied activity, and marvellous practical ability – when shall we see his like again? The world is poorer for his absence; a beautiful life is ended, a fair and shining light has been extinguished, and I mingle my tears with those of the children, the thousands of rescued children, who have lost a father and a friend. Earth is poorer, heaven is richer!

SALLY WESLEY
The Jewel in the Poet's Crown

6

Sally Wesley had had a hard day. Brought up in comfortable, even luxurious, circumstances, she was unused to the rigorous life style which her recent marriage to Charles Wesley in 1749 had brought with it. That day she had bumped along behind him on horseback for over fifty miles from Manchester, down through Stoke-on-Trent, to Stone in Staffordshire. Eighteenth-century roads could be treacherous, often miry and impassable, or filled with potholes large enough to drown a horse and man. Highwaymen roamed the countryside, ready to attack a lone horseman. So after the strenuous days she had spent accompanying Charles as he preached in towns and villages in the north of the country, Sally was thankful to arrive safely at an inn to rest for a night or two. Soon they would resume their journey south to their home in Bristol.

Slipping into the yard at the rear of the property, Sally found a quiet spot where she could relax for a short while. Here, in a tuneful voice enriched by her lilting Welsh accent, she began to sing softly to herself – a hymn of praise which sprang from a heart filled with thankfulness to God and to the One who had poured out his life for her sake and loved her with a changeless love.

Standing outside their home that evening, several young women were astonished to hear the soft sweet strains of a woman singing coming from the yard of the wayside tavern that lay immediately adjacent to their house. How different from the usual sounds of crude jests and laughter of travellers as they refreshed themselves with ale and whatever other fare their host provided! The girls stood transfixed as the melody flowed on. Then quickly they ran to call their father, the local vicar. Together they all listened in silence as the singer, oblivious of her audience, finished her hymn.

Sally Wesley was surprised to hear the landlord summoning her. Evidently, so he informed her, the vicar had called and was asking to speak with her. After complimenting the young woman on her voice and explaining that he had overheard her singing a few moments earlier, he asked whether she would consent to sing in his church the following day. Yes, Sally agreed, but a condition was attached. She was happy to oblige as long as her husband might preach the sermon. But when the vicar learnt that Sally's husband was one of the despised Methodist preachers, whose influence was being increasingly felt throughout the country, he hastily withdrew his invitation.

When Charles Wesley decided to ask for Sarah Gwynne's hand in marriage, in November 1748, he met with many obstacles. First he was over forty years of age, while Sally, as she was commonly known, was only twenty-two. Then he had undertaken never to marry without consulting his brother, John, and receiving his endorsement of the choice. This was by no means a foregone conclusion; but to his surprise when he mentioned the question of marriage he discovered that his brother had pre-empted him by having already selected three eligible young ladies who might suit Charles. Sally Gwynne was among them.

Sally's father, Marmaduke Gwynne, a Breconshire magistrate, was both wealthy and influential, while his wife, a shrewd business woman, had recently inherited a small fortune. Their home, known as Garth, a spacious country mansion near Brecon, in South Wales, had become a popular rendezvous for the early Methodists. In addition to the Gwynnes' own family of nine, the household included numerous servants, a private chaplain and a nurse for the younger children. Sometimes as many as twenty guests would be staying at a time, a circumstance that presented the itinerant preachers with a ready-made congregation.

Not many years earlier, Marmaduke Gwynne's attitude to the revival preachers had been very different. When Howell Harris, the young Welsh schoolmaster-turned-exhorter, first began to preach in Breconshire, Gwynne, with all his authority as a magistrate, was determined to arrest him and commit him to the local jail for causing a public disturbance. But the winsomeness and power of the message he heard moved the antagonistic magistrate so deeply that he begged Harris' forgiveness and invited him back to his home instead. Truly converted to God, Gwynne now used his considerable influence to support the preachers who came to his area, and before long his wife and other family members had also been converted.

Charles Wesley first visited Garth in the autumn of 1747, staying six days as he preached both in the area and to the household. There he met Marmaduke Gwynne's twenty-one-year-old daughter, Sally, for the first time. A bond immediately sprang up between them. 'You have heard me acknowledge,' he later confessed quaintly, 'that at first sight my soul seemed pleased to take acquaintance with thee.' Travelling on from there to Ireland, Charles could not forget Sally. Her earnest spirit and eager desire to hear him preach were never far from his mind. 'Why did eternal wisdom bring us together here, but that we might meet hereafter at his right hand?' he asked rhetorically in a letter to her written from Dublin. Perhaps Sally had expressed some doubts over her own spiritual standing, so now Charles exhorted her earnestly: 'Surely the will of God is your sanctification. Even now he waits to be gracious unto you.' With all the hazards of mob violence he encountered among his Roman Catholic hearers in Ireland, he feared he might never see her again, and so continued, 'and before I see you again (if ever I see you again upon earth) you will know your Redeemer liveth and will feel his peace and power within your heart. This is my earnest expectation and my constant prayer.'

Six hazardous months later, Charles once more crossed the Irish Sea and headed for Garth. Exhausted, suffering from toothache, cold and soaked through, he urged his horse ever onwards into Breconshire. He records the last hours of his journey:

The weather grew more severe. The violent wind drove the hard rain full in our faces. I rode till I could ride no more; walked the last hour and by five dropped down at Garth. All ran to nurse me. I got a little refreshment, and at seven made a feeble attempt to preach. They quickly put me to bed. I had a terrible night. Worse than ever.

But under the kindly attentions of Mrs Gwynne, and doubtless of Sally, his strength soon returned. 'Through the divine blessing on the tender care of my friends, I recovered so much strength that I read prayers and gave the sacrament to the family,' he noted. The following week he had sufficiently recovered from his exhaustion to set off on a further preaching excursion. Recording this in his journal, he added, 'Mr Gwynne and Miss Sally accompanied me the first hour.'

The increasing affection between Sally and the preacher-poet of the revival, afforded many opportunities for Charles to preach in South Wales. Expressing his growing love, he wrote, 'Never have I found such a nearness to any fellow creature as to you.' Soon Charles and Sally had established a regular time each day to meet together in spirit at the throne of grace, however far apart they might be. Wherever he journeyed as he preached up and down the country, thoughts of Sally filled Charles Wesley's mind. On her part, Sally was constantly concerned that he should care for himself properly. In her opinion he did not take enough sleep. 'You will allow me to commend myself,' Charles responded humorously to some piece of feminine advice, 'I have not lain on boards since I left you, and have slept most immod-erately till six every morning. This indulgence I impute to a friend who constantly attends my slumbers and hovers over me as my guardian angel.'

Confiding his feelings for Sally to his friend Vincent Perronet, vicar of Shoreham, he was encouraged to receive his warm approval together with encouragement to approach the Gwynne family and ask for Sally's hand in marriage. But it was with some trepidation that Charles Wesley journeyed into Wales once more, this time to make a formal proposal to Sally and to gain the approval of her parents. For there were several potential obstacles to his success. First, Charles had agreed with his brother, John, that he would pursue the matter no further if he met with any reluctance from either Sally or her parents.

But his fears were ill-founded. As far as Sally herself was concerned, she had only one pre-condition before agreeing to marry Charles. She loved to listen to George Whitefield's preaching; and knowing the doctrinal differences between her future husband and Whitefield, she stipulated that she wished to be allowed to hear him whenever he was in the area. Approaching Mrs Gwynne on the question of marrying Sally, great was his relief when she replied stoutly, 'I would rather give my child to Mr Wesley than to any man in England.'

More problematic, however, was the question of persuading Mrs Gwynne that he was in a position to support her daughter in a manner to which the young lady had become accustomed. Though an itinerant Methodist preacher with little regular income, Charles Wesley eventually suggested that he would try to raise £100 a year for Sally's support. This sum, at least double the stipend of many eighteenth-century clerics, met with Mrs Gwynne's approval. But how to raise it was another matter. John was anxious that his brother should not become dependent on the generosity of others, so placing himself in a position of compromise. He therefore calculated that this income could probably be funded from the royalties the brothers could expect for their writings. They had jointly published several books of Charles' hymns and some of John Wesley's sermons. But Mrs Gwynne was not happy with this proposal. Who could tell, she objected, whether the Methodists would not become totally discredited in future days, and then no-one would buy their publications?

At last when an impasse appeared to have been reached, Charles Wesley's friend, Vincent Perronet, intervened and wrote to Mrs Gwynne. He reminded her of the true goal of the Christian: 'Alas, madam, what is all the world and the glories of it? How little does this world appear to that mind whose affections are set on things above! This state, I trust, is what you are seriously seeking after.' Nor were his words mere theory, for he added, 'I have a daughter now designed for a pious gentleman whose fortune is not half that of our friend's, and yet I would not exchange him for a star and a garter!' With many further exhortations this good friend urged Mrs Gwynne to adopt a generous spirit towards the settlement, predicting that Charles Wesley's hymns would one day prove more popular than their limited circulation now indicated. He was confident, therefore, that Sally's welfare would be secure. This letter fulfilled all that its writer had hoped, and soon any objections to the marriage on the grounds of finance melted away.

Not only did Vincent Perronet intervene on Charles Wesley's behalf. Another friend, whose regard for Charles and for his ministry was warm and faithful, had an important part to play. The Countess of Huntingdon, second daughter of Earl Ferrers, had been born into one of England's oldest and most aristocratic families. Converted in 1739, her contribution to the evangelical revival, both through her personal influence and through her estate, was of primary importance. When the Countess learnt of her friend's difficulties she undertook to make up the shortfall if ever Charles Wesley's income dropped below the required £100.

And so the wedding day was fixed for 8 April 1749. But even to the end there were difficulties. 'Just as we were setting out for Wales my brother appeared full of scruples and refused to go to Garth at all,' recorded Charles nonchalantly in his journal for 1 April. With unusual self-control for a man with so volatile a temperament, he commented patiently, 'I kept my temper, and promised that if he [John] should not be satisfied there, to desist.' But things were not looking too promising and Charles confessed to 'a heavy heart' as they travelled towards Garth. Still expressing an unwillingness to agree to his brother's marriage, John annoyed Charles yet more by insisting on fulfilling a number of preaching engagements on the way, so delaying the arrival of the groom and his party until the day before the wedding. On their arrival, however, John's 'scruples' melted away and the marriage day dawned clear and bright. The account left by Charles in his journal makes strange reading today:

We crowded as much prayer as we could into the day. Not a cloud was to be seen from morning till night. I rose at four; spent three hours and a half in prayer or singing with my brother, with Sally, with Beck [Rebecca Gwynne, Sally's sister] . . . At the church door I thought of the jealous prophecy of a friend, 'that if we were even at the church door to be married, she was sure, by revelation, that we would get no farther.' We both smiled at the remembrance. We got farther. Mr Gwynne gave her to me (under God): my brother joined our hands. It was a most solemn season of love! Never had I more of the divine presence at the sacrament. My brother then gave out a hymn:

> *Raise our hearts to things on high*
> *To our Bridegroom in the sky;*
> *Heaven our hope and highest aim,*
> *Mystic marriage of the Lamb.*

He then prayed over us in strong faith. We walked back to the house, and joined again in prayer. Prayer and thanksgiving were our whole employment. We were cheerful without mirth, serious without sadness. A stranger . . . said, 'It looked more like a funeral than a wedding.' My brother seemed the happiest person among us.

Highly gifted musically both in playing the harpsichord and in singing, Sally was an ideal life partner for Charles. Gentle, cheerful and unselfish, she made few demands on him. Not many others could have understood or handled the vast mood swings of the poet who could on one day touch such depths of despair as to write:

> *Weary, burdened and oppress'd*
> *Stranger to delight and rest,*
> *How can I beneath my load*
> *Preach redemption in thy blood?*
> *Looking every fearful day*
> *To become a castaway,*
> *How can I in sorrow tell*
> *News of joy unspeakable?*

and only a few days later could exclaim:

> *In a rapture of joy*
> *My life to employ,*
> *The God of my life to proclaim:*
> *'Tis worth living for this,*
> *To administer bliss,*
> *And salvation in Jesus's name.*

Even the company of his young bride could not keep Charles Wesley back from touring up and down the country preaching. Mrs Gwynne asked him not to venture into Ireland anymore, for on several occasions he had nearly lost his life either in crossing the Irish Sea or at the hands of the vicious crowds who mobbed the Methodist preachers. But Charles could give no such commitment and, in addition, Sally was eager to accompany him there.

Before long Charles Wesley and Sally rented a small house in Bristol for £11 a year. A sharp contrast to her impressive family residence in Garth, it was, nevertheless, their first home together. An extant document written in Sally's neat hand detailing each item of furniture shows that she was a conscientious home-maker, but during the early months of married life Sally loved to accompany her husband whenever she could. And Charles was proud of the diminutive figure who clung on behind him as he rode up and down the country. 'All look upon my Sally with my eyes,' he wrote in his journal.

Despite her willing and cheerful spirit, Sally did not find life as an itinerant Methodist preacher's wife at all easy at times. Often she would be frightened: 'I was riding over Hounslow-heath with my wife behind me', wrote Charles, 'when a highwayman crossed the road, passed us, and robbed all the coaches and passengers behind us.' Sometimes Sally was plainly disgusted. In Leeds the gallery of the church was partitioned into two, making sleeping quarters for the visiting preachers. On one occasion one of these apartments had been let out to a number of vagrants, who would otherwise have been sleeping rough. To Sally's consternation she found she had to pick her away across the slumbering forms of these men to reach her own apartment. Having been brought up in sheltered circumstances, this experience shocked her and she would often recall it in after years.

Sally Wesley's days of travelling with Charles came to a temporary halt when she became pregnant with their first child during the late summer of 1749. Instead she contented herself with entertaining the Methodist preachers who visited Bristol, among them John Nelson, whom she described as 'humble, obliging, simple-hearted, who lived above the world; full of meekness and of holy love.'

One night at the end of January 1750 Sally and her husband were jolted out of deep sleep by a thunderstorm, 'unusually loud and terrible', as Charles was to record. Sally, who had a naturally fearful disposition, was terrified and the shock resulted in a threatened miscarriage. With no option but to walk to the doctor's house the following morning, they were caught in torrential rain. Drenched to the skin, Sally was exhausted by the time they arrived. Two days later she lost the baby.

The next day Charles Wesley's friend, William Grimshaw of Haworth, in Yorkshire, arrived in Bristol, but on a sorrowful occasion. His twelve-year-old daughter, Jane, who had been attending the Kingswood School in Bristol, had died three weeks earlier of a virulent infection. News travelled slowly at that time, and Jane had been buried for two weeks before a letter informing Grimshaw of her death reached Yorkshire. With hearts still sore from their own loss, Charles and Sally Wesley were well-placed to console their bereaved friend, and Charles reported in his journal for 4 February, 'I brought my friend Grimshaw home with me, comforted for his happy daughter' – a comment which demonstrates that in Wesley's view, Jane, though still only young, had been a true believer.

About this time Sally Wesley gained a friend who was to love her genuinely and deeply. The Countess of Huntingdon, whose financial intervention had facilitated Charles and Sally's marriage, often stayed in her Bristol home at Clifton. She had maintained a correspondence with Charles

Wesley with remarkable constancy since 1740 and now she took Sally too into her affections, loving her like a daughter. Each letter to Charles contained without fail a reference to Sally; 'My kindest and most enlarged wishes abound to Mrs Wesley', she would write. Sometimes she would invite Sally to stay with her during one of the preacher's long absences from home. When Sally became pregnant once more late in 1751, the Countess was most anxious about her health and concerned to know when her baby was due.

During 1752 Charles Wesley was travelling mainly in the north of the country for much of the year. Sally accompanied him as much as she could until the summer when Jacky Wesley, a delightful fair-haired child, was born. Sally had now turned twenty-six years of age, and Charles Wesley was forty-five. Because his preaching took him so far from home Charles relied on Sally's wisdom and practical good sense in caring for Jacky. With her lovely voice she would sing to her infant son when he cried, and as he grew older she amused him by teaching him various songs. Jacky had inherited his mother's musical gift to a marked degree and also his father's sense of rhythm; and at a year old he was able to sing in tune and tap out the rhythms of the songs his mother sang.

But the winter of 1753-54 proved a time of deep affliction for the Wesley family. First John Wesley fell ill and rumours spread that he had died. Alarmed, Charles saddled his horse and rode hastily to London, where he discovered his brother was indeed critically ill. He had not been in London more than a few days before several letters reached him in quick succession, addressed in a familiar hand. The Countess of Huntingdon was writing to tell Charles that Sally too was seriously ill having contracted smallpox. The Countess delayed her return to her Leicestershire home and, arranging for the best medical care available, nursed her needy friend herself, while Jacky was taken elsewhere, away from infection. Day after day as Sally lay dangerously ill the Countess cared for her and often sat with her at night as well, regardless of personal risk. Sally longed to see her husband, but with characteristic self-denial said little about it, knowing he was needed in London. But the Countess thought differently. She suggested to George Whitefield that he should go to London to care for John Wesley, and so make it possible for Charles to come home to see Sally.

Describing his anguish of mind as his wife's life hung in the balance, Wesley expressed his feelings in verse:

> *Can we of ourselves resign*
> *The most precious gift divine?*
> *With thy loveliest creature part?*
> *Lord, thou seest our bleeding heart.*
>
> *Dearest of thy gifts below*
> *Nature cannot let her go;*
> *Nature, till by grace subdued,*
> *Will not give her back to God.*

When Charles arrived back in Bristol, he gazed dumbfounded at his pretty wife. Her condition had so disfigured her face that he scarcely recognised her:

I came to Bristol by four. I found my dearest friend on a restless bed of pain, loaded with the worst kind of the worst disease . . . She had expressed a longing desire to see me just before I came, and rejoiced for the consolation; I saw her alive, but O how changed!

Vaccination against smallpox had not long been introduced into the country, and Sally, like many other Christians of the time, felt that the practice was morally wrong. Sometimes unsuccessful, vaccination in Sally's view was a form of gambling with life, although in fact it had already reduced the numbers of fatalities from smallpox significantly. So now Sally regarded her illness as a direct dispensation of providence and 'blessed God that she had not been inoculated, receiving the disease as immediately sent from him.'

Sally, who was still only twenty-six, gradually recovered, but it became evident that the pockmarks had so scarred her young features that she was to be forever robbed of her attractive appearance. She had aged twenty years in those few short weeks. So disfigured was she that even her friends failed to recognise her at first. The considerable age difference between Wesley and his wife was now scarcely noticeable. Throughout this trial Sally's faith remained steadfast. 'Nothing is worth living for but to enjoy and glorify our God,' she wrote to her husband, adding, 'O that this may be the end for which my life is lengthened.'

Still weak from her smallpox, Sally had a further heavy affliction to endure. Despite precautions, sixteen-month-old Jacky had contracted the illness. As his young son struggled for life, Charles Wesley poured out his anxieties and prayers in verse:

> *When thou didst our Isaac give,*
> *Him we trembled to receive,*
> *Him we called not ours, but thine,*
> *Him we promised to resign.*
>
> *Meekly we our vow repeat,*
> *Nature shall to grace submit;*
> *Let him on the altar lie,*
> *Let the victim live or die.*
>
> *Yet thou know'st what pangs of love*
> *In a father's bosom move;*
> *What the agony to part,*
> *Struggling in a mother's heart . . .*

Sally expressed her faith and resignation in these words: 'My heart yearns for him so, that I wish I could bear the distemper again instead of him: but he is in our great Preserver's hands, who cares for him.'

For a further eight days Jacky struggled on, but early in January 1754 this highly gifted child lost the battle. Charles, who was again away from home when his son died, once more found an outlet for his sorrows in verse:

> Mine earthly happiness is fled
> His mother's joy, his father's hope,
> (O, had I died in Isaac's stead!)
> He should have lived, my age's prop;
> He should have closed his father's eyes,
> And follow'd me to paradise.
>
> Those waving hands no more shall move,
> Those laughing eyes shall smile no more;
> He cannot now engage our love,
> With sweet insinuating power
> Our weak, unguarded hearts ensnare,
> And rival his Creator there.
>
> Farewell, (since heaven ordains it so),
> Farewell, my yearning heart's desire!
> Stunn'd with the providential blow,
> And scarce beginning to respire,
> I own, and bow me in the dust,
> My God is good and wise and just.

After Jacky's death Sally cut off a lock of his fair hair. Folding it carefully in paper she wrote in her neat hand: 'My dear Jacky Wesley's hair: who died of the smallpox on Monday, Jan.7th, 1754, aged a year, four months and seventeen days. I shall go to him but he never shall return to me.'

The Countess invited Sally to her own home for a period the following summer and was gladdened at her steady improvement in health. Charles continued to travel far afield, but always found time to correspond with to Sally. 'I am going to Lands End', he would write. 'Follow me with your prayers. I miss you every hour.' 'How fares my dearest Sally?' he enquired lovingly. 'I long to have you with me.' Reminding her of their wedding anniversary he wrote, 'Eleven years ago he [God] gave me a token of love in my beloved friend; and surely he never meant us to part on this side of time.' When Sally's birthday came round he would sometimes write, 'Blessed be the day my dearest Sally was born.'

When baby Martha Maria, whom they called Patty, was born in June 1755, no-one was quicker to celebrate the occasion than the Countess. 'I do rejoice in finding dear Mrs Wesley is so well and her little girl will by the blessing of almighty God be continued as a present from heaven to her,' she wrote. But Patty lived only a month before Sally and Charles once more grieved the loss of their child. At about this time Charles Wesley gave up most of his itinerant preaching, both because Sally needed him and because of his uneasiness at the course he feared the Methodist movement might take with its threatened separation from the Established Church.

Two years later, in 1757, another son was born – named Charles, after his father, who was by now fifty years of age. A daughter, Sarah, also known as Sally, joined the family circle in 1759.

As she had done with Jacky, Sally would sing and play her harpsichord to amuse her toddlers and quieten them when they cried. Before his third birthday, Charles, like the son she had lost, showed extraordinary musical talent, as he began to play the harpsichord himself, picking out by ear the tunes his mother sang.

When he had to be away from home Wesley would advise Sally on the care of the children. After his young son had been ill with measles he wrote: 'I was in hopes the worst was over with Charles. The whooping cough does not always accompany the measles, and will not, I trust in his case. The girl may not have them at all . . . If you can cast all your care upon him who careth for you, you need not wean your daughter . . .'

If Sally had a defect as a wife, it would be in her management of finances. Generous to a fault and coming from a
wealthy family background, she had constant difficulty in
learning to economise. Often the family was short of money.
'How does your money hang out?' Charles enquired in
one letter. 'As for me, I spend none and have none to
spend'. And from another letter it is clear that the family
was still in difficulties: 'Our first temporal is to get out of
debt,' comments Charles. Later letters suggest that Sally
may have received some legacy, so easing the financial
strains on the family.

In May 1760 another daughter, called Susanna after
her grandmother, was born. But this child's life too was
cut short at eleven months. Three years after Susanna's
death, in 1764, a baby whom they named Selina, after the
Countess of Huntingdon, was born. Sally was thirty-eight
by this time . But like Patty, this baby only lived for five
weeks. In 1766, when Charles Wesley was nearly sixty, their
son Samuel was born, and the following year a last child,
whom they called John James, was added to the family.

With three young sons, Charles Wesley entertained the
hope that one of them at least might some day be called to
take up the noble task of bringing the light of the gospel to
the people of England. But while his father was away
preaching in London, six-month-old John James was taken
ill. His battle against disease was short but distressing, and
the child had died before his father could be notified. Sally
wrote to Charles immediately:

This comes to acquaint you that our dear little babe is no
more. His agony is over; but it was a hard struggle . . .
But glory be to the Redeemer's love in declaring for the
consolation of distressed parents, that 'of such is the kingdom
of heaven!' O that I may arrive as safely in the harbour of
eternal peace!

On hearing of his infant son's death, Charles wrote immediately to his wife and also tried to book a seat on the next possible coach home:

'Father, not as I will, but as thou wilt. Thy will be done on earth as it is in heaven.' Let my dearest companion in trouble offer up this prayer with as much of her heart as she can: and God who knoweth whereof we are made, and considereth that we are but dust, will, for Christ's sake, accept our weakest, most imperfect desires of resignation. I know the surest way to preserve our children is trust them with him who loves them infinitely more than we can do.

In the event the child had been buried before Charles Wesley could reach home. Never was there a murmur of complaint from Sally that she had to cope with her sorrows alone. A further letter demonstrates the quality of her Christian faith. Speaking of John James, she wrote: 'The sufferings he went through are now at an end and he is eternally secure from the malice of men and devils. When I come to die I shall be thankful.' Sally's griefs had sharpened her longings for a better world beyond the afflictions of her present lot. But her confidence in the mercy and goodness of God never wavered as she continues, 'At present I can only say, "The Lord is righteous in all his ways and orders all things for the good of his children." May I be found among that happy number in that day when he makes up his jewels.'

Despite her meek resignation to God's will, however, this bereavement almost crushed Sally's spirit. Of the eight children she had borne five had died. In her distress she cried out to God to spare her the pain of following yet another child to an early grave. She was particularly concerned for eighteen-month-old Samuel, for a case of smallpox had just been confirmed in a neighbouring family, and the child could so easily have caught the infection. God heard Sally's prayer, and even more than this, he gave her an inner confidence that none of her three remaining children would be taken from her; a confidence she never lost, even when they succumbed to life-threatening illnesses.

Facts about Sally Wesley's later years are surprisingly few. After Charles had finished his itinerant preaching he also stopped keeping his journal, so details of his movements come mainly from secondary sources. Even his letters rarely specify the year in which they were written. Charles suffered frequent ill health and consequently his periods of depression intensified. Sally's bright personality must have brought him much consolation. In 1771 the family moved from Bristol to Marylebone, then a quiet suburb of London. A woman who owed her conversion to Charles Wesley's ministry insisted on lending the Wesleys a large and comfortably furnished home, free of charge. From here, at his brother John's request, Charles could oversee the Methodist work in London which was centred at the Foundery, in Moorfields.

Samuel, who was five when the family moved to London, had also shown remarkable musical talent. Sally preserved a valuable coin given to her son before his third birthday when he played his first tunes on the harpsichord. By the time he was six he was composing music which he set to words of Scripture. From their larger London home Charles and Sally could now give their sons the musical training which their remarkable gifts justified.

Like most Christian mothers, Sally looked eagerly for evidences of spiritual concern among her children. Sometimes she thought she could detect the dawning of a desire after God. 'Your mother tells me Sam is very seriously inclined,' wrote Wesley to his son Charles. His daughter too he described as 'much awakened.' But Charles and Sally were deeply disappointed that these early indications of interest seemed to fade away. The musical and literary circles among which the Wesley children moved appeared to rob them of much spiritual sensitivity. When the twenty-year-old Samuel embraced Catholicism to advance his musical career, his parents were devastated. His father, now nearing eighty years of age, blamed himself, recognising that a degree of parental pride in his sons' abilities had allowed the priorities in the home to become distorted. A long poem expresses his dismay and grief – sentiments which Sally must surely have shared:

> *But while an exile here I live,*
> *I live for a lost son to grieve,*
> *And in thy Spirit groan,*
> *Thy blessings on his soul to claim,*
> *Through Jesu's all prevailing name,*
> *Presented at thy throne.*
>
> *Shock'd at the hypocrites profane,*
> *My son, when undeceived, restrain*
> *From worse, if worse can be;*
> *Nor let him all religion cast*
> *Behind, and shelter take at last*
> *In infidelity.*
>
> *Patient till death I feel my pain,*
> *But neither murmur or complain,*
> *While humbled in the dust.*
> *My sins, the cause of my distress,*
> *I feel, and mournfully confess*
> *The punishment is just.*

Grieved that his children did not share his Christian faith, Wesley did not allow his sorrows to overcloud his joy without any relief. Celebrating the return of Sally's birthday, he could write:

> *Come away to the skies,*
> *My beloved, arise,*
> *And rejoice on the day thou wast born;*
> *On the festival day,*
> *Come exulting away,*
> *To thy heavenly country return!*

As the 1780s progressed, old age took an increasing toll on her husband's strength, and Sally knew well she could not expect him to continue with her long. In much weakness he called for Sally one day and asked her to write down some lines at his dictation:

> *In age and feebleness extreme,*
> *Who shall a sinful worm redeem?*
> *JESUS, my only hope thou art,*
> *Strength of my failing flesh and heart;*
> *O could I catch a smile from thee,*
> *And drop into eternity!*

In these, the last lines he was to compose, the poet-preacher cast the anchor of his soul on that same hope which had sustained him for fifty years since that first Whitsunday in May 1738. He spoke little in the last weeks of life. When Sally asked him if he wanted anything, he answered, 'Nothing but Christ.' As the end drew near she asked if he had anything to say to the gathered family. 'Only thanks! love! blessing!' responded the dying man. Grasping his errant son, Samuel, by the hand, he said in hope and faith, 'I shall bless God to all eternity that ever you were born. I am persuaded I shall.'

As 29 March 1788 dawned Sally could see her husband's life slipping away. 'Press my hand if you know me,' she begged. His response, though weak, satisfied Sally. 'Lord . . . my heart . . . my God . . .' he whispered. And later that day Charles Wesley left Sally and his family as he was given to know in experience that glory for which he had often prayed:

> *And through the shades of death unknown*
> *Conduct me to thy dazzling throne.*

John Wesley wrote quickly to his bereaved sister-in-law assuring her that as far as he was able, he would keep her from want. But one thing troubled him. He knew that Sally had never managed finances well. So now John wrote kindly to her:

My wife used to tell me, 'My dear, you are too generous. You don't know the value of money . . .' Possibly you may sometimes lean to the same extreme. I know you are of a generous spirit. You have an open heart and an open hand. But may it not sometimes be too open, more so than your circumstances will allow? . . . If your circumstances are a little narrower, should you not contract your expenses too? I need but just give you this hint, which I doubt not you will take kindly, my dear Sally.

John Wesley made as generous a provision for Sally as he could, stipulating that she should be paid an annual annuity for the rest of her life. But when her brother-in-law died three years later, Sally asked that all the capital might be realised. This she used until the sum was exhausted. In her later years she moved out of the large house in Marylebone to live in a smaller house in City Road with her unmarried children, Charles and Sally, who both earned adequate money to support their aged mother. For many years before she died she rejoiced in knowing that both these children had embraced the faith that she and Charles Wesley had held so dear. Samuel's life and behaviour, however, despite his outstanding musical attainments, grievously disappointed his mother.

At last in December 1822, at the age of ninety-six, this brave and consistent Christian woman was taken from the pain, weakness and sorrows of earth. All her life she had feared death, but now when confronted by its reality, Sally was no longer afraid. Sometimes in her weakness she would find it hard to pray, and then she would plead for the prayers of those who were caring for her. Ever conscious of her sins, she often folded her frail and wrinkled hands together and repeated many times over words from the Litany: 'By thy precious death and passion, good Lord deliver us';

adding, 'my only plea is "God be merciful to me a sinner".'
Referring to her mother's last days, Sarah Wesley wrote, 'Hers
was a trembling faith, but it was founded upon the Rock.'

During the last night of her life she repeated over and
over again, 'Open the gates . . . open the gates.' Falling
into a deep sleep, she woke suddenly, smiling. 'Are you
happy?' asked Sarah. 'Oh yes!' exclaimed the dying woman,
'Christ is indeed precious to me.'

These were her last words before those gates swung open
to receive her and the trumpeters of glory welcomed her to
that place her poet-husband had described as he concluded
a birthday hymn he had written for her many years before:

> *There, there at his feet*
> *We shall suddenly meet,*
> *And be parted in body no more;*
> *We shall sing to our lyres*
> *With the heavenly choirs,*
> *And our Saviour in glory adore.*

SAMUEL PEARCE
'Let the God of Samuel Pearce Be My God!'

7

A youth of sixteen sat writing alone in his room. Before him lay a copy of Philip Doddridge's *Rise and Progress of Religion in the Soul,* a book written some forty years earlier and rapidly becoming a Christian classic. Carefully copying down words from the book in front of him, Samuel Pearce wrote, 'Use me, O Lord, I beseech thee, as the instrument of thy glory; and honour me so far that, either by doing or suffering thy appointments, I may bring praise to thy name, and benefit to the world in which I live.' This petition formed part of a solemn covenant which Doddridge urged his readers to make with their God.

At last Samuel had finished. Page after page lay before him as he concluded, and ascribed the whole 'to the triune God in the presence of the angels and all the redeemed hosts of heaven'. But the boy was still not convinced that his self-dedication was sufficiently sincere or that the motives behind it were pure enough to please God. So, acting far beyond anything recommended by Philip Doddridge, he cut himself with a knife and sealed his consecration with his signature written in his own blood.

Born in 1766, Samuel Pearce was the younger son of a Plymouth silversmith. From a Dissenting family with a long Baptist tradition, he early heard stories of the courage and endurance of previous pastors of his church in days of intense persecution when to bear the label 'Baptist' was to court abuse and ill treatment. Of the 150 church members of the Plymouth Baptist Church when Charles II was restored to his throne in 1661, most faced the confiscation of their means of livelihood, crippling fines, imprisonment and banishment. Their pastor, Abraham Cheare, was banished for life to a small island in Plymouth Sound where he endured 'great inhumanities from merciless jailers' until set free from his bondage by death itself.

Samuel Pearce's parents and grandparents were loyal church members and devoted Christians. But the loss of his mother when he was little more than a baby meant that Samuel was brought up in his grandparents' home, five miles from Plymouth in the village of Tamerton Foliot. Here he lived until he was eight or nine years of age and attended the small Baptist Meeting House with his grandparents, who faithfully gave the child his early religious instruction. When he returned to his own home he attended the local school until he was thirteen and was old enough to learn his father's trade. But in spite of all his early religious advantages, Samuel showed little inclination to seek his father's God. Mixing with young people of his own age, he shrugged off any religious impressions which might stand in the way of his enjoyments, and at his own confession, set his heart so firmly on evil that had not the God of mercy preserved and restrained him from his chosen course, he feared he should have been utterly ruined.

Plymouth was an exciting place for an eighteenth-century youth. Alive with rumours of war and invasion scares, its shipyards were a constant hub of activity; sailors thronged the narrow streets, embarking or disembarking from the waiting warships. Their coarse company, flamboyant ways and tales of distant lands were enough to enthral any teenager. Conflict with France and Spain was a continual threat during Samuel's boyhood, and when he was thirteen Plymouth trembled as it learnt of the combined fleets of these two nations mustering for attack on the unprepared town. Driven back to sea by stormy weather, the fleets abandoned their planned invasion and prayers of relief and thanksgiving must have ascended to God from the small Baptist church.

But God's hand rested on the impressionable youth, and he could not cast off the demands of an unquiet conscience. When he was fifteen his father sent him to enquire after a sick neighbour. Entering the cottage, he discovered the man was critically ill, even dying. Seized with dark despair, he was crying out in an agony of foreboding, 'I am damned for ever, I am damned for ever.' Such words cut the listening lad to the quick and he could never forget them. He managed, however, to shake off their immediate impression on his mind and soon returned to his accustomed way of life.

On a hot July Sunday in 1783 the sixteen-year-old discovered that the preacher for the next two Sundays was to be a student from Bristol Baptist Academy, a man only two years his senior. Perhaps that very fact made Samuel Pearce attend to his messages with increased interest. But more than this, Isaiah Birt was a young man of tried Christian experience. Already he had suffered sorely for his faith at the hands of bullies in his own village in the Forest of Dean. Virtually buried alive by his cruel associates and then trampled upon until he only narrowly escaped serious injury, Isaiah Birt had steadfastly held fast to his faith and was now training as a candidate for the ministry.

The work of grace in Samuel Pearce's heart was quick and decisive. Describing it in later life he wrote:

I believe few conversions were more joyful. The change produced in my views, feelings and conduct was so evident to myself, that I could no more doubt of its being from God than my own existence. I had the witness in myself and was filled with peace and joy unspeakable.

When Isaiah Birt returned to Bristol the new convert felt the parting keenly. Reflecting the extent of his early religious training, Pearce wrote to him begging for his prayers:

Never forget me. Oh beseech God that he will ever keep me from a lukewarm Laodicean spirit! May my affections to a crucified Saviour be constantly on a flame. Religion makes a beggar superior to a king! What can equal the felicity of a Christian – the soul's calm sunshine and heart-felt joy? Nothing! Nothing!

Like a yacht in full sail before the wind, Samuel Pearce set out upon his new life as a Christian. One of his earliest acts was to make that covenant with God, promising 'from this day solemnly to renounce all former lords, world, flesh and devil, in thy name' and undertaking 'no more directly or indirectly [to] obey them'.

But all was not plain sailing for Samuel Pearce. Having resolved and engaged in this way to renounce all known sin and having sealed his serious intent in his own blood, he was distressed beyond measure to discover the pull that his own sinful nature still exercised over him despite all his resolutions. He had expected the resolve in itself would give him the strength to obey. Bewildered and brought to despair when he found himself falling short of his own standards, he began to search around for causes of his failure. As he thought of his blood-sealed covenant, he gradually understood that he was in fact relying on the strength of his own determination as a means of satisfying God, rather than casting himself on the blood and righteousness of the Saviour. With all the impetuosity and radicalism of youth, Pearce hurried up to his attic room, took his covenant and tore it to shreds, flinging all the scraps out of the window to be blown far away by the wind. His new understanding of the grounds upon which a sinner may stand before God, he expressed in verse:

Saviour, bind me to thy cross
Let thy love possess my heart;
All besides I count but dross
Christ and I will never part.

In his blood such peace I find,
In his love such joy is given,
He who is to Jesus joined
Finds on earth a real heaven.

On his seventeenth birthday Samuel Pearce was baptised as a believer in the Plymouth Baptist Church. Eight others were baptised at the same time, four of whom also bore the surname 'Pearce'. Either Pearce was a common name in the area, or alternatively the eager convert had already been influencing his own relatives to seek after a true saving faith.

From his earliest days as a Christian Samuel Pearce found an insatiable longing rising up within him to draw others to the kingdom of God. Shyly at first and only after much persuasion, he began to preach in the surrounding villages, and with such effect that his pastor, Philip Gibb, together with the church, came to the conviction that God was calling him into the ministry. Gibb offered to educate the young man in a wide variety of disciplines to prepare him for such a calling. All day long Pearce would toil in his father's silversmith shop, and each evening hurry to his pastor's home where he would spend many hours learning and reading. Here he developed habits of study which never left him.

1783, the year of Pearce's conversion, was also the year when the war of the American Colonies to gain their independence was at last concluded. Now Britain could no longer ship her convicts and criminals out to Virginia to toil on the plantations as she had done for almost a century. A fresh dumping ground for such unwanted citizens must be found, and Australia's Botany Bay, newly discovered by

Captain Cook, seemed an ideal location where trouble makers could conveniently be taken and forsaken. In May 1786 the first shipload of 750 men and women was due to set sail. Living in Plymouth, Pearce was quickly aware of the human cargo so soon to leave British shores for ever. Within this young man of twenty years of age welled up an overwhelming desire to join the convict ship himself, to fare as they fared, and to spend the rest of his days far from home if only he might win their souls for Christ.

And beyond that, yet another ambition was taking shape in his mind. He had heard of the uncivilised and often violent Maoris of New Zealand. Why should he not be the first missionary to that distant land? Many were the enquiries he made, unknown to his father and friends, as to how he might join the ship so soon to sail. But ignorant of the correct protocol, the young man failed in his endeavour and saw the convict ship slip out of Plymouth Hoe, while he himself was left behind on the strand.

Deprived of this means of service, Samuel Pearce continued to preach in the surrounding villages until it became unmistakably evident that he was called by God to a preaching ministry. Bristol Baptist Academy, at that time the only institution for the training of Baptist preachers, dated back some fifty years, and here it was that in the autumn of 1786 Pearce began his three years of training under the capable supervision of the principal, Dr Caleb Evans. Already some notable students had received their training at the Academy, men such as John Rippon, John Ryland, John Sutcliff and Benjamin Beddome. Robert Hall (Junior) lectured in philosophy and the classics, combining his work at the Academy with his position as assistant pastor at Broadmead Baptist Church.

A warm bond of friendship soon sprang up between Pearce and the younger Robert Hall, who was even at that time revealing his outstanding preaching gifts. With the privilege of attending his lectures and also hearing him preach, the student preacher was moulding and developing his own unique preaching style.

But neither his studies nor the commendations of his tutors robbed Pearce of his burning desire to seek the salvation of his fellow men. Sent out to preach in the villages around Bristol, he lost no opportunity to influence his hearers, many of whom, like Wesley and Whitefield's congregations in that area, were miners. Preaching for two consecutive Sundays at Coleford in the Forest of Dean, Pearce spent the intervening weekdays in study and his evenings in visiting the miners in their homes. This was the very village where Isaiah Birt had been so abused as a boy, and some of these men who listened to Pearce's preaching may well have been the bullies who had treated Birt so cruelly not many years earlier. Pearce himself describes the scene:

In a poor hut with a stone to stand upon and a three-legged stool for my desk, surrounded with thirty or forty of the smutty neighbours, I have felt such an unction from above, that my whole auditory has been melted into tears, whilst directed to 'the Lamb of God which taketh away the sin of the world'; and I weeping among them, could scarcely speak nor they hear for interrupting sighs and sobs . . . Indeed, had I at that time been at liberty to settle, I should have preferred that situation to any in the kingdom with which I was then acquainted.

With a further year left to complete in his college studies, Samuel Pearce received an invitation from Cannon Street Baptist Church in Birmingham to serve them during his college summer vacation. This he was glad to do, and the blessing which accompanied his weeks there led to a further invitation to come again at Christmas, and yet again to become the pastor of the church for a probationary year when his studies ended in the summer of 1789.

After serving the church for this probationary year, Pearce was ordained in August 1790. Men whose names would later be forever linked with that of the young preacher took part in the service: Dr John Ryland, soon to follow Caleb Evans as principal of the academy, came across from Northampton, and Andrew Fuller of Kettering preached the sermon. But it was not a foregone conclusion that Pearce would become the permanent pastor of Cannon Street. There were other strong pulls on his loyalty, for his own home church in Plymouth was anxious to draw him back. But after some hesitation Pearce, now twenty-four years of age, responded to the call from Cannon Street and began his permanent ministry there.

Contemporary records suggest that Samuel Pearce possessed considerable preaching gift. William Jay of Bath, an acute observer of his fellow preachers, has accorded to Pearce probably the highest accolade to which any preacher could aspire: 'When I have endeavoured to form an image of *our Lord* as a preacher, Pearce has oftener presented himself to my mind than any other.' Such a comment could not be accounted for by eloquence alone; far more significant was the impact of the man himself upon his messages, coupled with the evangelical earnestness that pervaded them. Commenting on Pearce's preaching style, Andrew Fuller, whose biographical sketch of his friend's life is considered among the best pieces to come from his pen, wrote:

His face was the face of a calm yet intense mystic. His eyes, like the hair, were a deep brown, the features refined, and the mouth very mobile. His address was easy, his voice pleasant, but sometimes overstrained in the course of a sermon. His delivery was rather slow than rapid; his attitude grateful, and his countenance a faithful index to his soul – his eyes beaming benignity, and speaking in the most impressive language his willingness to impart not only the gospel but his own soul also. He was known as 'the silver-tongued'.

But above all, it was the content of his messages that was of most importance. Continuing his description, Fuller wrote, 'Christ crucified was his darling theme from first to last. This was the subject on which he dwelt at the outset of his ministry among the Coleford miners, and this was the burden when addressing the more polished and crowded audiences in Birmingham.'

'Christ and him crucified', Pearce once said during a time of serious illness, 'is a religion for a dying sinner. It is all the most guilty and the most wretched can desire.'

But Samuel Pearce's ministry in Birmingham was far from trouble-free. Of a membership of 150, a number were hyper-Calvinist in their persuasion, and soon thought their new young preacher far too free in his offer of gospel mercies to the men and women in the pews before him. More than this, his demands that a professing Christian's life should be marked by vigilance and spiritual zeal agitated and annoyed some whose way of life was far below the standards now proclaimed from their pulpit. 'Absence from the Communion, swearing, lying, gross living and open sin' were among the issues that gave rise to his frequent rebukes both private and public. At last after eighteen months at Cannon Street, Pearce found no other way of cleansing the life of the church apart from a public excommunication of offending members. After such a catharsis the blessing of God came down upon the life of the church, and many were the conversions which gladdened the heart of their young pastor.

During these difficult months Pearce experienced one outstanding consolation – his marriage to Sarah Hopkins, a young woman from nearby Alcester whom he had met during his visits to Birmingham while still studying at Bristol Academy. Sarah had been brought her up in the shelter of a godly home. But like Samuel, she too had lost her mother at a young age, and on her had fallen much of the responsibility of helping in the home and caring for the younger members of the family. Already she had known a 'deep experience of Christ' which, as Pearce expressed it, 'added a tenfold strength to the bands of my attachment.'

Married to Sarah six months after his ordination, Samuel Pearce wrote quaintly and exultantly to a mutual friend:

The occasion of my writing is a source of joy inexpressible to myself – a joy in which I know you will participate. I am no longer a bachelor. Your amiable friend permitted me to call her my own yesterday. One dwelling now contains us both and St Paul's Square that dwelling. Pray that our union to each other may lead us to more communion with God himself.

But these joys also brought with them cares and anxieties, and when their first child, Louisa, was born the following year, Sarah herself nearly lost her life. Pearce's anguish as he considered the all-too-likely possibility of losing Sarah threw the young preacher upon the upholding grace of God. But it also showed him his own weakness. 'I shall never fear another trial,' he said afterwards. 'He that sustained me amidst *this flame* will defend me from every *other spark*.' And to Sarah herself he wrote, 'Oh my Sarah, had I as much proof that I love Jesus Christ as I have of my love to you, I should prize it more than rubies.'

Yet amidst all his domestic joys and concerns and the burdens of the pastorate, Samuel Pearce could never forget his first eager desires to become a missionary. Soon after he had settled in Birmingham he heard a sermon by Thomas Coke, the sixty-year-old Methodist leader, whose earnest zeal for missionary endeavour had involved him in crossing the Atlantic eighteen times – journeys undertaken in days when such travel was long and fraught with danger. That sermon, based on 'Ethiopia shall soon stretch forth her hands unto God' (*Psa.* 68:18), kindled the smouldering embers of Pearce's concern for unevangelised peoples,

[155]

raising it to a flame. It stirred him so deeply that from that moment he could say he had 'a passion for missions'.

Some years prior to Pearce's ministry at Cannon Street, a monthly gathering for prayer 'for the revival of religion and the spread of the gospel to the most distant parts of the habitable globe' had been instituted in response to the 'prayer call' of 1784 sent out by John Ryland, John Sutcliff and Andrew Fuller of the Northamptonshire Baptist Association. They in turn had been challenged and inspired by a small work known as *An Humble Attempt* (the opening words of a much longer title), by Jonathan Edwards, the New England theologian, published in 1748. After reading this treatise, demonstrating the close connection between united corporate prayer and the revival of God's cause world-wide, these three men had issued a call for 'a Concert of Prayer' such as Edwards, together with some Scottish ministers, had issued in 1744. All Christians were urged to meet together on the same day and time each month, though in their separate churches, to plead specifically for the revival of religion and the spread of the kingdom of God among all nations of the earth. This prayer meeting was well attended at Cannon Street, and Pearce did all in his power to foster its life and vision, spending many hours scouring all possible sources for information on the progress of missions and passing this on to his people to stimulate their praying and desire.

In April 1791 Samuel Pearce met for the first time one whose zeal for missions not only matched but exceeded his own – William Carey. The shoemaker-pastor from Moulton was already well-known to men such as Andrew Fuller and John Sutcliff. His *Enquiry into the Obligation of Christians to use Means for the Conversion of the Heathens,* soon to have so profound an effect upon the churches, was still only in manuscript form. Pearce, however, would have known of it because it had been written at the instigation and encouragement of one of his own deacons at Cannon Street four years earlier. Now in April 1791 Carey was moving to a new pastorate at Harvey Lane in Leicester, and Samuel Pearce was to be the preacher at his recognition service.

Here was a man of truly kindred spirit, and after the day's preaching was complete Pearce asked Carey if he would read his *'Enquiry'* aloud to the small group of men who had lingered behind. For some who listened, the concept that Christians had a duty to reach out to other nations with the gospel was quite new, but not for Pearce, who commented that Carey's theme only added 'fresh fuel to my zeal'.

A year later, in May 1792, when the Northamptonshire Association was meeting in Nottingham William Carey preached his historic sermon based on Isaiah 54, 'Enlarge the place of thy tent...lengthen thy cords and strengthen thy stakes', under those two much-quoted headings, 'Expect great things from God. Attempt great things for God.' Pearce was preaching elsewhere that day, but he would have quickly learnt of all that had taken place and of Carey's anguished plea to Andrew Fuller as the men were preparing to return their homes: 'Is nothing again to be *done*, Sir?' The plea was effectual and from that moment Fuller cast all his endeavours behind Carey's desire to reach out to the unevangelised peoples of the world. Pearce would have rejoiced to know that Fuller then proposed a date in the following October for the whole question of missions to be discussed by the Association.

Though not a member of the Northamptonshire Baptist Association, Samuel Pearce was one of the dozen or more men meeting in the back parlour of Beeby Wallis's small home in Kettering on 2 October 1792. At twenty-six years of age he was the youngest present apart from a theological student, a member of his own church, and he had journeyed the furthest to attend. That day, whose significance was scarcely known at the time to those few men present, saw the formation of the Baptist Missionary Society, its creation consecrated by a sacrificial offering of £13 2s 6d, some collected in Fuller's snuff box and some in pledges. Pearce himself promised one guinea – a substantial sum from his stipend of £100 per year. A quiet observer of all that took place, he commented, 'There I got my judgment informed, and my heart increasingly interested. I returned home resolved to lay myself out in this cause'.

Back in Birmingham the young preacher brought the needs of the infant cause before his church, stirring up their expectations and commitment to such an extent that within a few weeks he had collected an astonishing £70 to add to the funds – more than two thirds of his own yearly stipend. When the next meeting of the fledgling missionary society was held four weeks later, on 31 October, Pearce once again covered the seventy miles on horseback. But it was a dispirited group that met at Kettering that day, having had opportunity to reflect on the enormity of the task they had undertaken, and on their own limited resources. Carey was unable to attend and Fuller was ill, but when Samuel Pearce arrived bringing with him his £70, not merely in pledges but in actual donations, it 'put new spirits into us all'. With his contagious zeal, his pulpit gift, his Christ-like spirit, and as a bonus, his winsome appearance, it was clear that young Samuel Pearce would be an invaluable asset to the cause. He was promptly added to the executive committee joining Ryland, Sutcliff and Fuller.

With little more than a year left before Carey was to leave English shores for ever, a friendship of unusual depth grew up between him and Pearce – a friendship that increased rather than diminished in spite of a separation of many thousands of miles and poor communications. 'Oh how I love that man whose soul is deeply affected with the importance of the precious gospel to the idolatrous heathens!'

Pearce exclaimed of William Carey. Five years his senior, Carey embodied for Pearce all that was good and noble in Christian character. Writing to him shortly after he had arrived in India, Pearce was to say, 'Love for your person, respect for your character, joy at your prospects, gratitude for your communications, desire for your success . . . so variously affect me, that I can scarcely compose myself to write at all.'

Contemplating the manifold needs of the young missionary society, Pearce wrote to Fuller, 'I am willing to go anywhere and do anything in my power.' North and south he travelled, addressing meetings and always concluding with moving and urgent appeals for funds. A thankless task, it often resulted in abuse and miserly responses. Like Fuller, who shared the work of fund-raising with him, Pearce would sometimes feel like creeping into a back lane to weep at the meanness of the response. 'I think the Methodists more likely to succeed than you,' said one discouraging voice. 'I should feel more pleasure in giving them ten guineas than in giving you Baptists one.' But still the money came in. His own church at Cannon Street raised a further £127 10s 10d in 1793, totalling twice their own pastor's salary in just a year – a real personal sacrifice for many in the light of the harsh economic conditions of those years with Britain and France at war. Throughout the 1790s food prices climbed steadily, many basic commodities doubling in price between 1790 and 1795. Bread riots were common in Birmingham, with thousands needing financial relief merely to feed their families.

Preaching opportunities began to multiply for Samuel Pearce as he became well-known beyond his own immediate circle. In both London and the Midlands his ministry was sought after. Early in 1794 came an urgent invitation from Dublin, taking him across the Irish Sea to conduct an extended six week mission. Perhaps among the happiest days of his life, he saw considerable fruit for his ministry and doubtless much interest in the cause that lay nearer to his heart than any other. Commenting on this visit, a deacon in one of the Dublin churches wrote to a friend, 'We have had a jubilee for weeks. That blessed man of God, Samuel Pearce, has preached among us with great sweetness and much power.'

But another secret hope lay smouldering in the heart of the young preacher from Birmingham. Before Carey had sailed on the *Kron Princessa Maria* in June 1793 he had let slip a few words which Pearce could never erase from his mind. Recalling the occasion he wrote, 'I will never forget the manner of Carey's saying, "Well, you *will* come after us," and my heart said, "Amen".' Only six words, but they re-ignited a long cherished desire that he might one day become a missionary himself.

Many considerations seemed to militate against such a prospect. The work at Cannon Street was being remarkably blessed by God. Cleansed from the influence of unprincipled members, the church could record at least fifty conversions during 1794. Sarah, his wife, still far from strong, was now expecting a second child. But the most pressing argument of all for remaining in England was the vital role Pearce now occupied in publicising the work of the mission and raising funds. And yet despite all this, he could not suppress his urgent desire to devote the rest of his days to preaching the gospel in some distant land to men and women utterly destitute of any Christian truth. The more he tried to dismiss such aspirations, the stronger became their hold.

As the first letters from Carey arrived in England, telling of the unlimited needs of the Hindustani peoples, Pearce's longings gained momentum. In his private diary, he recorded his thoughts: 'Birmingham, fifty thousand people and ten evangelical ministers. Hindustan, twice as many *millions,* with not ten preachers. Why this disproportion? I must go, if others go not.' He began a serious study of the Bengali language. Few text books were available and his progress was painfully slow. Often he worked late into the night by the light of a candle. Sometimes his studies went well: 'Difficulties vanished as soon as encountered. Read and prayed; prayed and read. Made no small advance. Blessed be God.' But at other times he confessed, 'Found the Bengali difficult this evening, but captains and merchants master it for money-making. Ashamed I was so disheartened. Looked up to God and set about it with cheerfulness. Other duties always prevent my beginning until eleven o'clock at night.' And to Carey himself he wrote, 'I fear I shall be able to do but little to purpose for want of a tutor to teach me the pronunciation. Of one character in the Sanskrit pronouns I can find no account anywhere; you will tell me when we meet.'

Hopes and aspirations had now given place to a steady determination to join Carey in India if this should prove the will of God. To ascertain this, Pearce decided to set aside a whole month when he would give himself to seeking some sure indication from God of his purposes. One day each week was to be given to prayer and fasting. Extracts from his diary reveal the character and the spiritual struggles of this devoted Christian man. Beginning in the second week of October, he wrote:

Oct. 8 1794. With many tears I dedicated myself body and soul to the service of Jesus; and earnestly implored full satisfaction respecting the path of duty. I feel an increasing deadness for all earthly comforts; and derive my happiness immediately from God himself.

10. All prospects of pecuniary independence and growing reputation, with which in unworthier moments I had amused myself, were now chased from my mind, and the desire of living wholly unto Christ swallowed up every other thought

. . . my whole soul felt as if it were going after the lost sheep of the heathen.

11. I dreamed that I saw one of the Christian Hindus. Oh how I loved him! How pleasant it will be to sit down at the Lord's Table with our brethren and hear Jesus preached in their language.

24. The after part of this day has been gloomy indeed. All the painful circumstances which can attend my going have been laid upon my heart and formed a load almost insupportable . . . Whilst at a prayer meeting I looked around on my Christian friends and said to myself, 'A few months more and probably I shall leave you all.' But in the deepest of my gloom I resolved though faint, yet to pursue.

One major obstacle remained to prevent Samuel Pearce from offering his services to the other members of the committee as a missionary candidate: Sarah was far from willing to go. Her own health and that of her young family were clearly important considerations. So he prayed on, but scarcely dared discuss the matter with his wife. But one day the tension between his love for Sarah and his desires for missionary endeavour became so acute he could not conceal his oppression of spirit from Sarah any longer. Enquiring gently what was troubling him, Sarah did not need an answer – she had already guessed. The next words she spoke elated his whole being: 'I hope you will be no more uneasy on my account. For the last two or three days I have been more comfortable than ever [before] in the thought of going.'

But Sarah had a suggestion to make. She asked her husband to place every circumstance before the committee: his strong desires together with the many obstacles that seemed to obstruct the path to missionary service – and await their decision. 'If they advise your going, though the parting from my friends will be almost insupportable, yet I will make myself as happy as I can and God can make me happy anywhere.'

[162]

With exultant spirit Pearce took up his pen to write to Carey, intimating his hopes of soon joining him in India:

Yesterday my wife told me that on mature deliberation she approved of the plan I have adopted. Oh help me to praise God! It is a relief inexpressible . . . Oh how happy I shall be to sound the name of my dear Lord Jesus in the Bengali tongue on the plains of Hindustan. Give my dear love to Ram Bosu; tell him I long to take him by the hand and call him brother . . . In my next I hope I shall be able to ask you to 'prepare me a lodging'!

Nothing now remained but for Pearce to gain the approval of his church and then to lay the whole burden of his desires before his fellow members of the mission committee. The first proved more difficult than he had anticipated. At a special church meeting he told his people all his aspirations but warned them that though he would be glad to know their opinion, he could not be bound by it. He knew how they loved and respected him and feared that they might be unwilling to part with him. He was right. After much discussion amongst themselves the church begged him not to leave. Hearing that the decision was to be made by the mission committee the church members asked to be represented at the committee meeting by two of the deacons to voice the concerns of the church.

Steady now in his purpose, Pearce had still two more weeks of his month of special prayer. God's special presence during those days seemed a stamp of approval on all his aspirations. He recorded in his diary:

All was dullness – when of a sudden God smote the rock with the rod of his Spirit and immediately the waters flowed . . . An irresistible drawing of soul which far exceeded anything I had ever felt before, and which can never be described nor conceived by those who have not experienced it – all constrained me to *vow* that I would *by his leave*, serve him among the heathen . . . If ever in my life I knew anything of the

Holy Spirit, I did then. Hunger, fullness, cold, heat, friends, enemies, all seemed nothing before God. Christ was all in all. Many times I concluded prayer but was sweetly drawn back till my physical strength was almost exhausted. The more I am thus, the more I pant for the service of my blessed Master among the heathen.

Scarcely had he penned those words when a letter arrived from Andrew Fuller. Kindly and tenderly he wrote, but the letter was filled with objections to Samuel Pearce going to India. He could not be spared, so important was his contribution to the mission at home. Fuller had recently suffered a slight stroke which had left his face partially paralysed. He and many others hoped that Pearce would be able to step into his position of leadership at a future date if the occasion arose. And then two days later came another letter, this time from John Ryland, who voiced the same objections. Puzzled and dismayed, Pearce could only comment, 'If my brethren knew how much I pant for the work they could not withhold their ready acquiescence. If I stay in England I doubt whether I shall ever know inward peace and joy again. Lord, I am oppressed: undertake for me.'

Fierce was the inward struggle in Pearce's heart over the next few days as he contemplated the real possibility that his colleagues might deny him the opportunity he so desired:

Striving to reconcile myself to whatever may be the decision of my brethren. I look at Brother Carey's portrait as it hangs in my study. I love him and long to join his labours. Every look calls up a hundred thoughts, all of which inflame my desire to be with him. *One thing I have resolved. If I cannot go abroad, I will do all I can to serve the Mission at home.*

By 7 November 1794 Pearce's special month of prayer was over. Four days later he travelled to Northampton to hear the verdict of the other members of the committee. They had been summoned by Fuller in these words: 'That dear man of God, Samuel Pearce, is resolved to go to India if his brethren in the ministry will give their consent. He requests that a day of prayer and fasting be set apart by the committee when he promises to open his heart and be directed by our advice'. On 12 November they met together in response to Fuller's invitation.

After spending the morning listening to Pearce's viewpoint, they spent the afternoon deliberating while Pearce and his two deacons passed the hours in prayer in an adjacent room. At last, with time at a premium, the men who had met to discuss Pearce's future emerged and handed him their decision in writing. It was unanimously adverse. They declared themselves fully satisfied with his qualifications for missionary service, but added that he could not be spared from the work in England – at least not for the present. Those final words were probably added to mitigate the pain of their decision for the eager young man, still only twenty-eight years of age.

With Christian submission Pearce did not attempt to argue against the outcome. Like Abraham he was prepared to offer up that 'Isaac' which embodied for him all the future purposes and blessings of God in his own life. A letter written to Sarah the next day indicated his willingness to accept the result of the committee's deliberations as the will of God:

I am disappointed but not dismayed. I ever wish to make my Saviour's will my own. My dear brethren have treated the matter with as much seriousness and affection as I could possibly desire and I think more so than so insignificant a worm could expect. Pray take care of their decision which I enclose. It will serve me to refer to when my mind may labour beneath a burden of guilt another day.

Only a few weeks later three-year-old Louisa, Samuel and Sarah's older child, was taken seriously ill. Away from home at the time, Samuel wrote to his wife: 'Repinings?

No we will never repine. Even if she die let us submit till we come to heaven: if we do not then see it is best let us then complain. Did God cheerfully give the holy child Jesus for us and shall we refuse our child for him?'

Spared this additional sorrow, Pearce continued to grieve in private over the death of his prospects of serving his God in India. He could not bring himself to write to Carey for a further four months and not before he had some more encouraging news to share:

My very dear Brother, Instead of a letter you perhaps expected to see the writer; and had the will of God been so he would at this time have been on his way to Mudnabatty . . . Full of hope and expectation as I was when I wrote to you last . . . I must submit now to stand still and see the salvation of God. Judging from the energy of my feelings, together with their long continuance and growing strength, I scarcely entertained a doubt but that I should this year go to assist you.

But to cheer Carey he was able to add that two more students from Bristol Academy had volunteered for missionary service and would soon be on the way to India. He also mentions that he was continuing with his studies of Bengali. Clearly the hope lingered on that he might yet himself join Carey. Carey's reply to this letter, though it must have made his disappointment yet more poignant, was also full of consolation and encouragement:

Oh my dear Pearce, had you come in reality when your mind was so intensely set upon it, methinks a greater happiness could not have befallen me. I know your disposition and your zeal for the Lord Jesus so well, that I conclude such a help is necessary to stimulate and excite my languid mind to action. But the welfare of the churches, conscience, honesty and reason forbid it. I must no more expect to see your face until I see you at the great day of the Lord. However, we are one, nor can rolling seas interrupt that unity of heart, which I trust we feel. We are both labouring in the same cause, and both serving under the same Captain, only with this difference; you are employed in the centre of the army and I am set to force an outpost of the enemy. Let us both be faithful unto death, and account it glorious even to die in such a cause.

Never allowing his disappointment to affect his Christian service, Pearce continued his busy schedule of preaching at Cannon Street, travelling the length of the country in the interests of the mission, and helping other missionary candidates to prepare for their long journeys overseas. To this he added a further labour: he began gathering materials for a work to be entitled *The History and Present State of Protestant Missions.* But the setback he had sustained affected his health, and the following year he experienced a period of extended illness. A letter to Fuller written as his health began to return reveals no alteration in the depth of his concern for India:

Through mercy I am almost in a state of convalescence. May my spared life be wholly devoted to my dear Redeemer! I do not care where I am, whether in England or in India, so that I am employed as he would have me: but surely we need to pray here that God would send more help to Hindustan.

To Carey, however, Pearce expressed himself with an openness reserved for a close friend. Even eighteen months after the decision had been made, the burden of his disappointment still weighed heavily on his spirits.

I fear that I shall never see your face in the flesh: but if anything can add to the joy which the presence of Christ and perfect conformity to him will afford in heaven, certainly the prospect of meeting with my dear brother Carey there is one of the greatest. Thrice happy would I be if the providence of God would open a way for my partaking of your labours, your sufferings and your pleasures on this side of the eternal world, but all my brethren here are of the opinion that I shall be more useful at home than abroad, and I, though reluctantly, submit. My heart is at Mudnabatty, and at times I even hope to find my body there, but with God I leave this. He knows my wishes, my motives, my regret . . . But I must be thankful that he allows me to stand sentinel at home. May I have grace to be faithful unto death.

With pleasure approaching rapture I read your last accounts. Blessed be God. Go on my dearest brother! God will do greater things than these. Already the empire of darkness totters and soon it shall doubtless fall. Do not fear the want of money. God is for us and the silver and the gold are his; and so are the hearts of those who possess it. I will travel from Land's End to the Orkneys but we will get money enough for all the demands of the mission. I have never had a fear on that head. A little exertion will do wonders.

With all the trust that deep friendship engenders, Pearce, though so far away, continued in this letter to confide his spiritual struggles to Carey: his fears that God may have rejected him, his reluctance for private prayer, and the barrenness of his heart in prayer and his struggles with pride. In conclusion he wrote: 'Oh my brother, I need your prayers and am greatly comforted that you do not forget me.'

Pearce's personality combined the contemplative and the active to a remarkable degree. Self-searching, spiritual devotion and desires for communion with God were blended with a life of constant activity and service both in his own pulpit and in his service for the mission. Nor did he neglect the needs of Sarah and the children for by 1797 the family had increased to four all under the age of six. Forced to spend a considerable amount of time away from home, he found the hours long that he was parted from Sarah and the family. Her prayers and support were a vital factor in all his Christian service: 'Pray for me, my dear, dearest friend,' he would plead, 'I do for you daily. O wrestle for me that I may have more of Enoch's spirit.'

'I shall be labour-proof and weather-proof for at least another thirty years,' wrote Samuel Pearce as he approached his thirtieth year, and looked on into the future, contemplating the years God might allow him for service to the church of Christ. Never robust, Pearce nevertheless enjoyed reasonable health, though his incessant toil and midnight studies of Bengali must have taken their toll. But his long journeys on horseback or in gigs with insufficient protection from the elements often meant arriving at his destination cold and wet. Once in December 1797, as he travelled between Shepshed in Leicestershire and Nottingham, Pearce was exposed to wind and rain for so long that he caught a severe chill. Recovery was slow, and throughout the following year even the slightest exposure to inclement weather would bring on a recurrence of his symptoms.

Pearce, however, had one particular joy at this time. William Ward, a young printer and newspaper editor from Derby had for some time been drawn towards Christian service, and for the last year had been studying under Dr John Fawcett in Yorkshire. There he had been encouraged to consider missionary work. He may have met Pearce some years earlier, but certainly he did so when he applied to the Baptist Missionary Society to go to India to assist Carey. An immediate bond sprang up between the two men, and Pearce was one of the preachers at Ward's formal acceptance by the society at a meeting in Kettering in October 1798. Ward, who together with Joshua Marshman was to become one of Carey's most trusted and important helpers in future days, commented that the preaching he heard that day 'set the whole meeting in a flame'. Pearce's passionate appeals might well have resulted in 'a cargo load [of missionaries] immediately', reported Ward.

Returning from Kettering, Pearce preached at Market Harborough in Leicestershire the following day, and then rode back to Birmingham together with a close friend of his. But on the way both men were caught in heavy rain, and forced to travel the remaining distance in wet clothing. In the evening Pearce was hoarse, and by the next day his former symptoms had flared up again. Though only thirty-two years of age, he seemed unable to shake off the debilitating effects of this cold. Thinking that 'pulpit sweats' might effect a cure, he tried to maintain his schedule of preaching at Cannon Street and among the villages in the vicinity of Birmingham. But the effort cost him dear, and soon his lungs became so inflamed he could hardly speak. Clearly in need of help, Pearce wrote to William Ward urging him to come to Birmingham to assist him:

Do you want time? You shall have it here. Books? You shall find them here. A friend? Be assured that the hand that moves this pen belongs to a heart warmly attached to you. If you love me, come and help me. Come and secure the hearts and the prayers of hundreds of Birmingham Christians, who only want to know you and love you too.

Ward stayed with Pearce and his family for three months, witnessing at first hand the zeal, love and spiritual devotion that characterised Pearce, though so unwell. To a friend he wrote:

Oh, how does personal religion shine in Pearce! What a soul! What ardour for the glory of God. You see in him a mind wholly given up to God; a sacred lustre shines in his conversation: always tranquil, always cheerful. It is impossible to doubt the reality of religion if you are acquainted with Pearce. I have seen more of God in him than in any other person I have ever met.

On 2 December 1798, six weeks after the service at Kettering, Pearce felt well enough to attempt to preach to his people once more. He took for his text the Angel's words to Daniel, 'Oh man, greatly beloved, fear not, peace be to you. Be strong, yea, be strong!' A sermon his people never forgot, it proved to be Pearce's last. Scarcely able to talk at all after so great an effort, he wrote to a friend saying that he thought his 'next ascent would be not to a pulpit, but to a throne – a throne of glory'. The next time his people saw him in his own pulpit was in February when he struggled to add a few words of comfort and challenge after the visiting preacher had concluded his sermon. He told them that amidst his great weakness his chief comfort lay in the hope of meeting so many of them in a better land, while his chief distress was the dread of having to testify against others who had heard his preaching yet rejected God's offers of grace and mercy.

During those days of illness, the thought of his family distressed Pearce most of all. To John Ryland he admitted: 'But my family! Ah, there I find my faith still but imperfect. However, I do not think the Lord will take me away till he helps me to leave my fatherless children in his hand, and to trust my widow also with him.'

Trial fell heavily upon trial for Samuel and Sarah Pearce that month. Sarah was expecting her fifth child at any moment, and when the little one was born in March she became critically ill once more. For days her life hung in the balance, while the four older children each succumbed to a fever. In the midst of all these anxieties, Pearce's doctor broke to him the news that he feared his condition was tuberculosis. The only hope for his life lay in travelling south to his home in Plymouth, where the weather conditions would be more favourable. As Sarah recovered strength he agreed to go, but the needs of the newly born child together with those of the other children prevented her from accompanying him – a separation both found painful to bear.

Far from the mild weather he might have expected in Plymouth during April, wintry conditions seemed unwilling to relinquish their grip and any hoped-for relief appeared a distant prospect. Though scarcely able to speak in anything more than a husky whisper, Samuel Pearce was not idle, and from that sickroom flowed letters: to Sarah, to his friends, his church, to John Ryland, Andrew Fuller and many others. These letters, some the most beautiful ever penned by a dying Christian, form Pearce's best memorial.

Early in May 1799 a valedictory meeting was to be held for the new missionaries soon to leave for India, among them Pearce's friend, William Ward. How he longed to be well enough to travel to Olney to join in that occasion! As the time approached it became increasingly evident that this was out of the question, for his condition was rapidly deteriorating. 'Unless the Lord work a miracle for me I am sure that I shall not be able to attend the Olney meeting,' he wrote to Fuller. In the event, he wrote to Ward, 'Alas! I shall see you no more. I cannot be at Olney on the 7th of May. The journey would be my death. But the Lord whom you serve will be with you then and for ever.' And to the meeting he addressed a letter which was read aloud at the close, drawing many tears from those who were present:

Happy men! Happy women! You are going to be fellow labourers with Christ himself. I congratulate – I almost envy you; yet I love you and can scarcely now forbear dropping a tear of love as each of your names passes across my mind . . . Long as I live my imagination will be hovering over you in Bengal; and should I die, if separated spirits be allowed to visit the world they have left, methinks mine would soon be at Mudnabatty, watching your labours, your conflicts and your pleasures, while you are always abounding in the work of the Lord.

And as the ship, *Criterion,* carrying the missionaries to India passed by Plymouth on 1 June, Ward could hardly bear to think of his friend lying so close at hand and so ill. In his private journal he confided his grief:

Oh my God! What would I give for the restoration to health of Brother Pearce! Oh, if it is possible, spare, oh spare his precious life! If I could have walked on the water I would have made long strides to Plymouth to-night, and laid his dear aching head on my throbbing heart.

Another man was also grieving on that June Saturday. As Andrew Fuller rode back from London where he had gone to accompany the outgoing missionaries, his mind was preoccupied with thoughts of Samuel Pearce. Not given to expressing his depth of emotion, Fuller wept much of the way home. He knew more than most what Pearce had meant to the mission, of the irreparable loss his death would mean both to himself and his colleagues, and the warm attractive quality of his Christian devotion. But nearing Kettering, his tears began to give place to prayer as he cried out many times over, 'Let the God of Samuel Pearce be my God!'

Meanwhile, making no significant recovery in Plymouth, Pearce longed to be back in Birmingham with Sarah and the children and to have his beloved church members nearby. So early in July the invalid set out on what was to be a long slow journey home. Able to travel only short distances at a time, it was five days before he reached Bristol. Here he rested at the home of John Ryland and his wife for several days before travelling on to Alcester where Sarah's sisters cared for him for a further day or two before he was able to attempt the last twenty miles into Birmingham.

Twelve more weeks of suffering lay ahead for Samuel Pearce. But precious weeks they were: for Pearce himself, as the brightness of the Celestial City shone upon him with increasing radiance; for Sarah, as together they were able to prepare for the separation that lay ahead; and for the church of Jesus Christ, both then and now, for so eminent an example of the grace of God to a dying Christian.

Scarcely able to whisper without intense pain, Pearce grieved that he could not speak to his wife and children and could only express his affection in warm embraces and loving looks. But Sarah wrote down some of the whispered words and exhortations he made to increase her confidence in the purposes of God however dark the circumstances. One morning as she enquired how he felt he replied, 'Very ill, but unspeakably happy in the Lord, *my* dear *Lord Jesus.*' Seeing her grieving he said tenderly, 'Oh my dear Sarah, do not be so anxious, but leave me entirely in the hands of the Lord Jesus, and think if you were as wise as he, you would do the same by me. If he takes me, I shall not be lost, I shall only go a little before: we shall meet never to part again.'

Spiritual darkness sometimes clouded his sense of the presence of God. To Sarah he admitted, 'I have been in darkness two or three days, crying, "Oh when wilt thou comfort me?" But last night the mist was taken from me and the Lord shone in upon my soul. Oh, that I could speak. I would tell the world to trust a faithful God. Sweet affliction! Now it worketh glory – glory!' And then he turned to comfort Sarah, 'O trust the Lord! If he lifts up the light of his countenance upon you as he has done on me this day, all your mountains will become molehills. I feel your situation, I feel your sorrows; but he who takes care of sparrows will care for you and my dear children.'

Towards the end as his pain increased he was able to say but little. The words he managed to articulate demonstrated deep thankfulness for all the mercies of God in his weakness and need. 'Oh how good God is to afford some intervals amidst so much pain! He is altogether good. Jesus lives, my dear, and he must be our consolation.' After a restless pain-filled night, he answered Sarah's enquiry about how he felt with these words: 'If it were not for strong confidence in a lovely God I must sink; but all is well. Oh blessed God, I would not love thee less. O support a sinking worm!' And again he said, 'Why should I complain?

My dear Jesus' sufferings were much sorer and more bitter than mine.'

On 10 October 1799 Samuel Pearce came at last to the end of the journey. Both he and Sarah knew it was the end, and he seemed to be given and unusual joyfulness of spirit that day. She repeated to him the words of John Newton's hymn:

> *Since all that I meet shall work for my good,*
> *The bitter is sweet, the med'cine is food.*
> *Though painful at present, 'twill cease before long,*
> *And then, oh how pleasant, the conqueror's song.*

'*The conqueror's song,*' repeated the dying man with a smile of delight. Perhaps he could already catch the strains of the anthem of heaven and the distant sound of trumpets as the angels of God prepared to welcome him home. And with these words he left behind his pain for ever. He was thirty-three.

Hearing of his death, Andrew Fuller exclaimed in a letter to Sarah:

'Oh Jonathan, thou wast slain upon thy high places! I am distressed for thee my brother Jonathan'. Oh that we all may emulate him! Try while your heart is warm to draw his character. Write all you can remember of him. Memoirs of his life must be published: he is another Brainerd.'

And John Ryland, whose chose the adjective 'seraphic' to describe his friend, preached at his memorial service, saying, 'I never saw at least in one of his years such active ardent zeal together with such gentleness, modesty and deep humility.'

For Sarah stormy years followed. Two of her five children were taken from her by death soon after their father. Despite all her sadness, she was yet able to say, 'I have not the least disposition to think hard thoughts of God. I wish to love and adore him.' But, understandably, Sarah's bereavements sometimes made her wish to 'hide herself where none could see her.' After a brief widowhood lasting only five years, she herself was taken from all her sorrows to join Samuel in that land where 'his servants shall serve him, and they shall see his face.'

If Samuel Pearce could have looked into the future, he would have rejoiced with a full heart to know that his own son, William, would one day become an accomplished printer and join William Ward in India, serving as his father had longed to do. Anna, his second daughter, was to follow her brother to India five years later to help with the education of Indian girls, and in time she married Jonathan Carey, youngest son of her father's great friend. She became the mother of S. Pearce Carey whose biography of his grandfather, William Carey, stands as the classic work on that great missionary.

Though the purposes of God behind Samuel Pearce's brief life span must take their place among the 'secret things that belong unto the Lord our God', we may say of a certainty that the prayer he offered as a boy as he inscribed his early covenant with God was answered a hundredfold. He had indeed been made 'an instrument of God's glory by both doing and suffering his appointments' – not to his own generation alone, but to many subsequent generations of the Christian church through the written records of his life and testimony.